Gospel Intimacy in a Godly Marriage

Gospel Intimacy in a Godly Marriage

A Pursuit of Godly Romance

Alan Dunn

PILLAR AND GROUND PUBLICATIONS

Gospel Intimacy in a Godly Marriage

Published by Pillar and Ground Publications,
a department of Publicaciones Aquila
5510 Tonnelle Ave.
North Bergen, NJ 07047–3029

First edition: 2009

ISBN: 978-1-932481-19-8

Printed in USA

Acknowledgments

I have written this book from sermons that I preached to married couples at a couple's conference in October 2003. I thank Pastors Steve Hartland, Stan Gray, and Murray Wilson of The Trinity Reformed Baptist Church, Baltimore, Maryland, who gave me the privilege to minister on that occasion and who warmly received my efforts. Pastor Eugene Pinero, of Iglesia Bautista Reformada, North Bergen, New Jersey, urged me to put these sermons into writing. I thank Pastor D. Scott Meadows of Calvary Baptist Church, Exeter, New Hampshire for his helpful encouragement. I am especially indebted to Pastor Jeremy Walker of Maidenbower Baptist Church, Crawley, England, for his editorial advice.

I am grateful to the people of God in Grace Covenant Baptist Church, Flemington, New Jersey. They have faithfully prayed for me through the course of this project. They have also prayed for you, the reader, that this study might benefit you and enable you to glorify our Lord Jesus Christ.

My children, Ethan, Elliot, Jeremy, and Andrea continue to delight my heart. I hope my marriage to their mother will be a testimony of the gospel that will speak to them for the rest of their lives. I am most grateful to the wife of my youth, Tricia, for whom I have written this book.

When my children were younger, I would often hug them and ask, "How come I love you so much?" I taught them to answer, "Because God is teaching you to love me." I thank my Lord Jesus Christ who is teaching me how to give His love to my wife. If Tricia and I can go to our graves having loved each other with His “gospel love” then our marriage will have served as a witness to Him who first loved us.

Table of Contents

Preface 11

PART ONE:

NAVIGATING THE JOURNEY INTO MARITAL INTIMACY

Introduction 15

1. The Doctrine Of God Directs Our Journey Into Marital Intimacy 17

Being intimate and the being of God

We are "the image of God"

Unified plurality

The picture of perfection

Jesus' language of "oneness"

2. The Doctrine Of Creation Directs Our Journey Into Marital Intimacy 28

The needs inherent in creation

The earth needs man's labor

The man needs the woman

The man named the woman

What God has joined together

3. The Doctrine Of The Fall Directs Our Journey Into Marital Intimacy 36

The essence of death is separation

Fig leaf rebellion

Divine justice

Divine Grace

A propensity to perversion

4. The Doctrine Of Redemption Directs Our Journey Into Marital Intimacy 49

A showcase for the gospel

A signpost to glory

PART TWO:

MARITAL INTIMACY AND THE GRACE OF GOSPEL LOVE

Introduction 57

5. The Challenges To Gospel Love 58

The intimacy we need: "Love me."

The privacy we want: "Leave me alone."

The invading conscience

The love that overcomes sin

6. The Enemy Of Gospel Love 68

Not any old love will do

Gospel realism: "Yes, that is sin!"

7. Be A Gospel Lover 77

The loved lover

Love with love

A disposition of forgiveness

A disposition of forbearance

8. The Transaction Of Gospel Love 84

An exchange of gospel commodities

Confession offered

Repentance expressed

Forgiveness bestowed

No vengeance

I promise

PART THREE:

OVERCOMING CHALLENGES TO MARITAL INTIMACY

Introduction 107

9. The Challenge Of Headship And Submission 109

Leadership: not "source"

Submission: not egalitarianism

Christ – the model of headship and submission

10. The Challenge Of Selfishness 130

The attitude of Christ

Discipleship and self-sacrifice

Wisdom from above

11. The Challenge Of Unbiblical Communication Patterns 141

Meaningful words

Cleansing words

Affectionate words

Sexual communication

12. The Challenge Of Unavoidable Death 153

Married to my wife

Married to my sister

Discipleship – "Until death do us part"

A society of love

Even so, come Lord Jesus

Notes 167

Preface

In the first part of this study, I will lay down some foundational perspectives. We will spend some time considering the doctrine of God, the early chapters of Genesis, and some foundational realities that pertain to marriage. Considering the foundational issues will challenge us. Although this is not an "academic" study, we will be required to think hard about deep truth. Unless we think about biblical truth, we will not have the biblical wisdom necessary to live that truth out in practical ways in our marriages. After we work through some foundational issues, we will see how the gospel teaches us to love our spouse, especially as we contend with our sin which so readily threatens our intimacy. We will conclude our study by considering how to overcome some practical obstacles to marital intimacy. There are many practical obstacles to intimacy. I have selected four: the challenge posed by our culture's confused and rebellious notions of authority; the challenge posed by our inclination to selfishness; the challenges involved in communicating biblically; and the challenge posed by the approach of death.

Throughout the study, we will be asked to think and to act biblically. With *renewed minds,* we would *present* ourselves to God to *prove His good and acceptable and perfect will* (Romans 12.1-2). Thinking and acting biblically is necessary if we would grow in marital intimacy and enjoy marriages that glorify Christ Jesus, our Lord.

My "target audience" is Christian couples. I realize, however, that unmarried singles might read this book as well. I would ask my single brothers and sisters to remember that I am addressing married couples. The single reader will read some statements that may sound a bit imbalanced, and may cause him to wonder whether I give biblical legitimacy to the single state. I assure you that I do. To include the teachings of Jesus and Paul on singleness would be to exceed the limits of this study. My focus is that special intimacy known to couples in marriage, specifically Christian couples. In my zeal to extol marital intimacy, I express myself in a manner that will no doubt sound extreme. This is because I am extremely convinced of the wonderful blessings which Christ gives to those couples who strive to obey His Word in their marriages.

My vantage point on our subject is decidedly masculine. My perspective on marriage is that of a husband and I speak, more often than not, to husbands. The husband is particularly called to cultivate marital intimacy. He is charged to love his wife (Ephesians 5.22-33). Were we husbands to love our wives with "gospel love," our marriages would be characterized by greater intimacy. Obviously, intimacy will not be achieved without the engagement of the wife, but the command to love is explicitly given to the husband. I speak to Christian couples, but I especially address the husband. So, gentlemen, I am giving you advance notice!

PART ONE:

NAVIGATING THE JOURNEY INTO MARITAL INTIMACY

Introduction

The pursuit of marital intimacy involves a paradox. When, as a couple, we begin to achieve genuine marital intimacy, we discover that we still are not fully intimate. Yes, we are increasingly intimate, but in many ways, we are still strangers. We know each other, but there is more to learn of each other. The journey to marital intimacy takes a lifetime and even by life's end we will not have reached perfect intimacy. Yet it is a journey begun only by those who already enjoy some genuine intimacy. That is the paradox: you must be genuinely intimate if you would grow in intimacy because, however intimate you are, you are not as intimate as you could be!

Let me liken the journey into marital intimacy to an ocean voyage taken by ancient mariners who must navigate by the stars. There are four guiding stars by which we navigate this journey into intimacy. Like the sailors of old, we must keep these four guiding stars before us. This journey is fraught with unexpected storms, the winds and swelling waves of which would threaten to bring our journey to a tragic, premature end. Sometimes we must sail through dark, disorienting fogs which obscure our vision. At other times, the sun's glare blinds us on those calm and cloudless days when it feels like we are dead in the water, still, not moving. We must beware of those dangerous currents which can capture our ship and thrust us off course. We will also face challenges that arise on board the ship, when the crew is not working well together, when the rigors of a sailor's life tempt us to quit and jump ship. Nevertheless, in crisis or in calm, we cannot lose sight of these four navigational points of reference.

The four guiding stars by which we can navigate the journey to marital intimacy are: the doctrine of God; the doctrine of creation; the doctrine of the Fall; and the doctrine of redemption. These four points of reference will help us to navigate the marriage vessel. They will provide us with a compass on our journey, help us to stay on course, and guide us to our God-glorifying harbor.

The discussion questions are intended to help in a small group or Adult Sunday School Class.

Discussion Questions for the Preface and Introduction

1. In order to appreciate the author's perspective, who is the "target audience," and from what "vantage point" does he write?

2. What is the "paradox" mentioned in the Introduction?

3. What are "the four guiding stars" by which to navigate a journey to intimacy?

1

The Doctrine of God Directs our Journey into Marital Intimacy

Being intimate and the being of God

The first guiding star on the journey to marital intimacy is the doctrine of God. God is the one supreme unifying truth: *for from Him and through Him and to Him are all things. To Him be glory forever. Amen* (Romans 11.36). If we are to understand this most private, personal, subjective experience called marital intimacy, we must begin by considering this most transcendent, objective reality: *in the beginning, God* (Genesis1.1). We should begin our journey into marital intimacy *in the beginning,* by orienting ourselves to *God*.

The being of God explains why we naturally seek intimacy. Marital intimacy is something much more wonderful than mere biological mechanisms or animal urges. Evolutionists suggest that our inclination to intimacy is simply an animal instinct to reproduce, or the male tendency to dominate, or just raw hunger for sensual pleasure. Not so. Our inclination to intimacy is essential to our being: we are creatures made in the image of God. Our created being reflects God's divine being.

WE ARE "THE IMAGE OF GOD"

Notice the first few words of Genesis 1.26 as God our Creator resolves to fashion man in His image. *Then God said, "Let us make man in our image according to our likeness.*" This singular, solitary God expresses Himself with a plural self-consciousness: *Let us make- in our image - in our likeness.*

Some scholars suggest that these plural pronouns are "majestic plurals:" a construction in the Hebrew language that communicates the idea of greatness, abundance, or majesty. Others say that here God is addressing His heavenly angelic court and that God made man to image His angels in heaven. These scholars point to God's ancient name, Elohim, which is a plural term that can refer to angels. In Psalm 8.5 we learn that man was made a little lower than the *elohim,* or lower than the angels. But are the plural pronouns in Genesis 1.26 simply a grammatical construction or a passing reference to angels?

I understand Genesis 1.26 to be a record of a conversation among the Persons of the Triune Godhead. *Let us make man in our image according to our likeness* are words of God's eternal decree which express His purpose for creating. We stand on holy ground, peering into the inner workings of the Triune Creator God. In Genesis 1.1 we read of God's singularity: *in the beginning God created the heavens and the earth*. But notice verses 2 and 3: *and the earth was formless and void and darkness was over the surface of the deep and the Spirit of God was moving over the surface of the waters. Then God said, "Let there be light and there was light.*" The first three verses of Scripture point to the Trinity. We can see God the Father in verse 1, the Spirit of God in verse 2, and the Speech of God in verse 3. John emphasizes God's Speech in John 1.1-3. *In the beginning was the Word and the Word was with God and the Word was God. He was in the beginning with God. All things came into being by Him. Apart from Him nothing came into being that has come into being.* The Speech of God is none other than *the Word which became flesh and dwelt among us* (John 1.14). The Speech of God in Genesis 1 is the Word of God in John 1 who is none other than the pre-incarnate Son of God whom we know to be our Lord Jesus Christ. *The Spirit of God* who is *moving over the surface of the waters* is the Third Person of the Godhead. *God* in Genesis 1.1 refers to the person of the Father.

UNIFIED PLURALITY

This tri-unity in God's being explains who and what we are, because He made us to be like Him. We are made in the image of this Triune God. We are what we are because God is who He is. If we are to understand who and what we are, we must begin by understanding something of the God who is our Creator. We are the image of this one singular God who is three persons with a unified plural self-consciousness.

Now notice Genesis 1.27. Both males and females reveal the image of God: *And God created man in His own image. In the image of God He created Him, male and female, He created them.* This is a form of Hebrew poetry. Moses writes poetically to underscore that this verse is important. He repeats his words for emphasis to get our attention. Moses uses this poetic form of writing to alert us to something immensely important: we, as male and as female, are the image of God. God images Himself in our specific genders: male and female. Humans are not asexual beings. We are either male or female, and it is as sexual creatures that we image God. Our sexuality is not essentially a matter of biology, psychology, or sociology: our sexuality is essentially a matter of theology. If we are to understand the marriage of two image-bearers we must begin with the doctrine of God. Have you ever thought that human sexuality is essentially theological? Our distinct genders, male and female, marvelously reflect the actual being of God.

What does marriage tell us about the being of God? When the two *become one flesh* (Genesis 2.24) they mirror the one singular God who is yet plural as the Trinity. The two, a plurality, become one, a unity. Our sexual plurality (male and female), unified in marriage (one flesh), images the very being of God. The Triune God is the divine plurality in unity. The male and female united as one flesh in marriage is the creaturely plurality in unity. God's unique being is manifest in marriage as the two *become one flesh*.

The picture of perfection

Sexual intimacy is the creaturely emblem of that intimacy which is known among the persons of the Trinity. Although marital intimacy involves much more than physical intimacy, physical intimacy is, perhaps, the epitomizing expression of what it means to be a plurality in unity: the two become *one flesh*. Moses gives us an implicit sexual picture in Genesis 2.24, 25: *for this cause a man shall leave his father and his mother and shall cleave to his wife and they shall become one flesh. And the man and his wife were both naked and were not ashamed*. Moses tells us that they were *naked*. This is discreet sexual language. He is delicately pointing at the physical union of the first couple. Elsewhere in the Old Testament, to *look on someone's nakedness* implies some form of sexual activity (cf. Leviticus18.6ff). When Moses tells us that *they were both naked,* he is politely speaking of their sexual union, physical intimacy without shame. There is no sin to separate them. There is total transparency. In Genesis 2.24-25 we see the completed picture of God's *very good* creation which reveals and displays His glory. Moses takes a snapshot of the image of God, male and female, set against the backdrop of a pristine creation.[1] As we gaze on this picture, we see the man and his wife together in intimacy, reflecting God's own being. Their one flesh unity is the human counterpart to the tri-unity of their Creator God. Behold the image of the Triune God, male and female, placed in dominion over creation, wrapped together in the oneness of sexual union.

The first couple's sexual intimacy also demonstrates their intimacy with God and their embrace of His purposes. In unified intimacy with each other and with God, they align themselves with God's created order and arrangement. As one flesh they give themselves to the tasks which God has assigned to them, carrying out those tasks as one flesh. By their intimacy, they will provide companionship for each other. By their intimacy, they will *be fruitful and multiply, and fill the earth*. By their intimacy, they will carry out what theologians call 'the dominion mandate,' and *subdue and rule over* the earth. If the man and the woman are to fulfill God's purposes in creation, they must be intimate.

Here is the reason a man leaves his father and his mother: to take his place in this marvelous picture, to glorify God by imaging Him in the dignity and wonder of sexual intimacy. What a beautiful picture! Here is the *very good* creation of God, glorifying Him, imaging Him in the regal splendor of the united couple who are exercising dominion over the earth. Everything is in order, and everything glorifies God.

Of course we must expand the meaning of intimacy to include much more than the mere act of physical intimacy. One flesh union involves all that we are in our gender-specific humanity. I am not a male merely in a physical way: I also have a *male* psyche and *male* emotions. So it is with a female. It is in our total body-and-soul maleness and femaleness that we knit together in physical and spiritual intimacy.

My intimacy with my wife should reflect that intimacy which the persons of the Godhead know. Think about that for a moment. If I am not intimate with my wife, then I dishonor my God. If I am not intimate with my wife, then I do not reflect God properly. My intimacy with my wife directly affects my ability to be intimate with my God. Peter tells me to live with her in an understanding way and to honor her as a fellow heir of the grace of God. Why? *So that my prayers may not be hindered* (1 Peter 3.7). I cannot properly commune with my God if I am not communing intimately with my wife. As couples, we do not properly image God if the 'plurality in unity' of our marriage is out of alignment. God's honor is at stake in our marital intimacy.

Today we see unprecedented attacks on marriage. In defense of marriage, many Christians employ pragmatic arguments, citing statistics to appeal to the practical benefits of marriage: the psychological benefits, sexual benefits, benefits to children, economic benefits, and social benefits. Americans are a practical people. We value what works. However, as compelling as those statistics are, we are to value something greater than our own personal benefit. Our "chief end is to glorify God and to enjoy Him forever."[2] We do not justify marriage because we can amass statistics that show how we benefit from marriage. Such an approach is too selfish and centers on man, not God. The basis of marriage is the doctrine of God, not the doctrine of man. In marriage, we should glorify God and enjoy Him. God is Himself the reason we marry and should stay married.

JESUS' LANGUAGE OF "ONENESS"

Jesus uses the language of 'oneness' to describe how He relates both to His Father and to us. By speaking like this, He gives us insight into the subject of intimacy. He says in John 10.30, *I and the Father are One*. *One* is the same word that Moses used when he described the intimacy of the first couple and said *they shall become one flesh*. Now, I do not mean to imply by pointing out this common use of the term *one* that the Father relates to the Son in a sexual way. The Father relates to the Son in a divine way. We will not fathom the depth of their relationship. Nevertheless, the divine oneness known by the Father and the Son is what we reflect in the *one flesh* nature of our marriages. Our *one flesh* intimacy involves more than our physical "flesh," it is a unity of all that we are, body and soul. Notice Jesus' words in the "high-priestly" prayer of John 17. He says in verses 20-23:

> *I do not ask in behalf of these alone, but for those also who believe in Me through their word; that they may all be one; even as Thou, Father, art in Me, and I in Thee, that they also may be in Us; that the world may believe that Thou didst send Me. And the glory which Thou hast given Me I have given to them; that they may be one, just as We are one; I in them, and Thou in Me, that they may be perfected in unity, that the world may know that Thou didst send Me, and didst love them, even as Thou didst love Me.*

Jesus uses the language of oneness. He describes the relationship of the Father and the Son as a mutual permeation of persons. Embedded oneness characterizes the love between the Father and the Son. The Father now gives that love which He has for His Son to us who are in Christ. We, in Christ, are to image that same love in our marriages. I can only point at the loving oneness found in the Godhead and ask you to think about Jesus' words.

Jesus describes our communion with Him and with the Father with this language of oneness in John 14.20-23.

> *In that day you shall know that I am in My Father and you in Me and I in you. He who has My commandments and keeps them, he it is who loves Me and he who loves Me shall be loved by My Father and I will love him and will disclose Myself to Him. Judas, not Iscariot, said to Him, "What then has happened that you are going to disclose yourself to us and not to the world?" Jesus answered and said to him, "if anyone loves Me, he will keep My word and My Father will love him and We will come to him and make our abode with him.*

Here Jesus speaks about the communion that we enjoy with the Father. It is a communion which is similar to the communion which Jesus enjoys with the Father.

Jesus says the Father is going to *disclose* Himself to us, and that we will experience a mutual indwelling: *you in Me and I in you*. Jesus is again describing oneness: plurality in unity. The Father and the Son, through the ministry of the Spirit, will live with us in intimate unity. The two, the Lord and the disciple, become one. The Lord indwells His disciple by the Spirit and is embraced within the disciple's very soul. As His disciple, I receive His love and respond with a transparent love, a love not unlike marital love, a love that is *naked and not ashamed*. The Spirit enables me to receive Him by unzipping my soul, unclothing myself, opening my heart, and standing naked and transparent before Him. I remove all coverings. I demolish all barriers. I clear away all obstacles. Nothing is to prevent us from genuinely indwelling each other. As His disciple, I am to be so filled with the conscious presence of Christ that I cultivate, not a singular consciousness, but a plural consciousness. I am to be so indwelt by the Spirit, so filled with a sense of communion with Christ, that I only know myself as defined in union with Him. I am to live with a conscious, immediate, continuous awareness of His presence. I live in Him and He lives in me. We are always together. I am not thinking of myself properly unless I am thinking of myself in immediate relation to Him who indwells me.

Now, I do not mean to be irreverent, but what Jesus describes here has much in common with marriage. He speaks of knowing and loving me in a way that reminds me of how I am to know and love my wife. As a married man, I do not have an accurate view of myself if I define myself apart from my wife. I must cultivate a plural self-awareness. I do not act as an 'I' but as a 'we.' Whatever I do, I do united to her. I am one flesh with my wife. She lives her life in me and I live my life in her. The only other persons who live in such interpenetrating unity are the persons of the Godhead.

We could easily become mystical when we ponder the immense spiritual and theological significance of marriage. My marriage depicts the very being of God. My marriage is a manifestation of my theology. The very nature of the triune God determines the nature of my marriage. In many ways, my embrace of my wife signifies my embrace of God. I am not saying that marriage is divine or that my wife is my god. I am not saying that I worship her. I do not have a little shrine with candles burning in front of her picture. But as I embrace her in obedience to Scripture, I also embrace God's purposes for me as a married man. My willing embrace of His purposes for me in marriage is the result of a deeper heart-embrace of God Himself. As I embrace her who is defined as 'image of God,' I embrace God's purposes for me in my marriage. My embrace of her is a theologically significant embrace.

We are, by definition, theological beings: we are 'image of God.' We are creatures who manifest God, not least in our sexuality. We are His image as male and female, husband and wife. We, by grace, have come to know and to love the Triune God. Our love for God moves us to embrace our spouse in the awareness that we are mirroring His plurality in unity. He loves Himself and us with an infusing intimacy and we should likewise love Him and our spouse intimately. Our marriages should reflect the very being of our God as we learn to live as one flesh, each spouse saturating the other as the two become one. He has brought us into the mystery of being one flesh. It is in our marital intimacy that we will glorify God and display the wonder of the God who is One God in three persons. The more completely intimate I can be with my wife, spiritually and physically, the more I will glorify my God.

Discussion Questions for Chapter One:
The Doctrine of God Directs Our Journey
Into Marital Intimacy

1. What is the ultimate explanation for why we naturally seek intimacy?

2. What is the nature of God's being and how is His being reflected in marriage?

3. What is signified by "the picture of perfection" seen in Genesis 2:24-25?

4. How does Jesus' relationship to the Father instruct us in our relationship to Jesus as His disciples and in our spouse as married believers?

5. Sum up how it is that marriage is "theologically significant?"

2

The Doctrine of Creation Directs our Journey into Marital Intimacy

THE NEEDS INHERENT IN CREATION

God created us to be intimate. It is contrary to God's purposes for anything in creation to exist in isolation, disconnected and detached. Creation is a living fabric, a throbbing tapestry of interwoven threads. God has stitched creation together so that the intertwining threads give and receive life from one another. Every part of creation interconnects and contributes to every other part. Nothing exists isolated and alone. God made every single thing with an innate need to connect intimately to some other created thing. Unified connected components are found in biology, chemistry, physics and sociology. There is an inherent inclination in every single thing to gravitate toward and to unite to its complimentary components which together fit into the living tapestry of creation. When the various elements of God's creation are in their proper place, each thread intimately intertwines with those other threads with which God made it to live. Each individual part gives and receives that which God designed it to give and receive. Thus God stitches the living fabric of creation together into the unity of life. Order, integration, unity: such is the nature of created life made to reflect and to glorify the Creator Himself.

Each individual part needs to assume its place and fit into God's created order. God has designed every individual part to both receive what it needs and to give what is needed so that life is sustained as a unified integration of all its parts. This arrangement of having to satisfy mutual needs is not due to any defect in creation, nor is it the result of sin and the Fall. God created the world as this living tapestry of intertwined components, each receiving and contributing what God has purposed for its own fulfillment and for the benefit of the larger creation. Thus the needs of the individual component are met as that component meets the needs of those other components to which it is connected. God arranges everything in creation so that each individual part has its needs met as it serves to meet the needs of the other parts of creation to which it is connected. We can speak of "creation needs." Nothing is disconnected but "needs" to be vitally attached to creation in its proper place, functioning as God designed.

In Genesis 1.2 there are three "creation needs" which God then satisfies through the course of the creation week. *And the earth was formless and void, and darkness was over the surface of the deep; and the Spirit of God was moving over the surface of the waters*. Moses tells us of three "creation needs:" emptiness, formlessness, and darkness. The empty world needed to be filled. The formless world needed to be shaped. The dark world needed to be illuminated. The nascent creation was in need of inhabitants, shape, and light. Over the course of the creation week, God met those needs in reverse order. First, He created light, and 'satisfied' the need of the darkness by giving it its complementary partner: light. Next, He created boundaries, and thus met the need of formlessness. Finally, He created the inhabitants whom He designed to live within those boundaries, and thus He filled the need of the initial emptiness.

The earth needs man's labor

Genesis 1.1 through 2.4 forms a literary unit, an introduction, in which Moses introduces us to the creation as a whole. The next literary unit (Genesis 2.5-5.1) concerns the Fall. In chapter 2, Moses sets the stage for the Fall by introducing us to the man who, for a time, lives alone as the image of God.[3] He exercises leadership (later called 'headship'), over the earth and the animals before the woman's arrival, and he continues to exercise leadership after her arrival. Our interest at this point is in the 'creation need' that God designed the man to meet. Genesis 2.5-6 informs us that God made the man to meet a creation need inherent in the earth itself. Now no shrub of the field was yet in the earth, and no plant of the field had yet sprouted, for the Lord God had not yet sent rain upon the earth. And there was no man to cultivate the ground. But a mist used to rise from the earth and water the whole surface of the ground.

God made the earth to be in need of the man's labor. The earth had no man to *cultivate* it. God made the earth having the need to be cultivated by man. God satisfied this need when, in verse 15, *the Lord God took the man and put him into the Garden of Eden to cultivate it and keep it*. The earth was designed to receive the impress of the man's labor. As man functioned as a noble worker, imaging God who created all things, the earth then met his needs and bore life-sustaining fruit. Moses uses the same word, *cultivate,* in verse 15 as he did in verse 5. The man was also *to keep* the ground. The man, through his labor, was knit into the ground as part of the tapestry of creation. In fact, the man's union with the earth became an aspect of the definition of the man. He is *Adam* which means "red earth." God joined the man to the earth. The man would not become who he was made to be apart from his living connection to the earth. He sustained that connection through his labor. The earth naturally responded to the impress of the man's work. As the man knit himself into the earth through his labor, the earth produced the food which sustained his life. The man takes his place and images God, working as God intended. The result is an ordered, unified, living showcase for the glory of God.

The original creation needs were met by the creation of light, boundaries, and inhabitants. The man was made and met the creation need of the ground. Now we learn that the man also had creation needs which God met by creating his complement: the woman.

The man needs the woman

In Genesis 2.18, we learn what creation need the man had which God met by creating the woman. *Then the Lord God said, 'It is not good...'* We have probably read this verse so many times that we just read across those words. But those words should feel like a huge speed bump. Thcsc words jar our axles. What is Moses saying? Something is not good? Seven times in the first chapter we read: *the Lord saw it was good*, with the culminating *it is very good* of Genesis 1.31. The Creator judged His creation to be *very good*. But now we are reading along in the second chapter and come to verse 18 – bang! Here is something which is not good? That is jarring!

What is not good? *It is not good for the man to be alone; I will make a helper suitable to him*. The man, while alone, was already exercising leadership and obeying part of "the dominion mandate" of Genesis 1.28. He was already exercising *rule* over the earth. He was ruling by cultivating and keeping the ground. But the man was to rule, not only by his labor, but also with his words. So God brought all the animals to the man. The man, living in sinless though undeveloped unity with his Creator-Father, understood not only God's words, but God's actions. God's actions are revelatory and the man correctly interpreted what His acts meant. The man, God's image, was to imitate God, to act like God. When God brought the animals to the man, he acted as God intended him to act: he exercised rule over the animals by giving them names. He understood that God was placing the animals under his dominion and stewardship. He assumed responsibility for the animals by naming them. Like his Creator-Father who spoke creation into existence and *upholds all things by the power of His Word* (Hebrews 1.3), the man also defined the world with his creature words. Like the words of his God, his creature words had authority. Whatever he named the animal was the animal's name. Once Adam named an animal, the name was not to be changed. Yet this exercise of regal rule only intensified the man's experience of being alone. He did not find among them one *suitable for him*.

The man named the woman

The man's need had become acute. It was not good for him to be alone, so God met his need with one suitable for him. The woman would be his partner and knit intimately with him to complete God's purposes for His image-bearers in the tapestry of life. When God brought the woman to him, Adam rightly interpreted God's action and imaged God in a distinctly masculine way. He exercised leadership with his words by naming the woman, giving leadership to her, and assuming responsibility for her. As soon as God brought the woman to Adam, he named her.[4] With his words he gave her significance, meaning, and definition: *this is now bone of my bones and flesh of my flesh; and she shall be called Woman, because she was taken out of man*.

Observe that the woman corresponded to the man physically. Adam defined her in physical union with himself: she was *bone of my bone, and flesh of my flesh*. Although she was different from him, she was also a refashioning of him. God took Adam's rib and fashioned the woman from it and then brought her back and joined her to him again. She was independent of him, but at the same time united to him. She was an independent creature designed to be intimate with him. She was made of his bones and his flesh. She was not merely an appendage that was to attach externally to Adam. God joined her to Adam as though He were putting that rib back in place again. *This is now bone of my bones and flesh of my flesh*. Here are words that echo the depths of that intimacy known among the Divine Persons of the Trinity. The God who is plurality-in-unity is glorified as His image names His image: *she shall be called Isshah: woman*.

'Isshah' is the feminized form of man: 'Ish.' Notice, ladies, Isshah did not say, "No, no, no, I do not like that name. I will not have that name." *Whatever the man called a living creature, that was its name*. Her name was 'Isshah' because Adam, in the exercise of his headship, named her. This exercise of loving Godlike rule was integral to the man's distinctive masculinity. He knew her accurately and defined her in the unity of their shared being. They were made for intimacy. They were made for sexual intimacy, for total one-flesh intimacy.

Moses sees our first parents in the pristine beauty of their oneness and says, *for this cause a man shall leave his father and his mother and shall cleave to his wife, and they shall become one flesh. And the man and his wife were both naked and were not ashamed* (Genesis 2.24-25). This is why a man leaves Dad and Mom. The bond of a father, the bond of the mother, and the friendship of a sibling, are all lesser loves surpassed in the pursuit of marital intimacy. He leaves because his 'creation need' is met in his wife.

What God has joined together

The only intimacy that exceeds marital intimacy is that to which Christ summons us when He calls us to be His disciples. Indeed, being married is like being religiously devoted. "Marriage is to human relations what monotheism is to theology."[5] It is a leaving of all others to be devoted to one supreme, intimate love.

When Jesus taught on marriage in Matthew 19.4-6, He referred to Genesis 1.26. First He asked, *Have you not read that He who created them from the beginning made them male and female?* Then He quoted from Genesis 2.24, "*for this cause a man shall leave his father and mother and shall cleave to his wife and the two shall become one flesh. Consequently they are no longer two but one flesh*". His application? *What therefore God has joined together, let no man separate*.

As surely as God brought Eve to Adam, so too, by divine providence, God brings to each one of us our particular husband or wife. Sometimes we wonder, "Could I have married someone else? Is there not someone else out there with whom

I could be intimate?" Such a question is a denial of divine providence and an insult to love. To love is to fulfill the horizon of your gaze with the one loved, not to pop up your head, look about, and wonder if there could be somebody else. God has brought your spouse to you and you have embraced each other in vowed commitment. You have become one flesh. To ask whether there could be someone else is to speak as a stranger to true intimacy. Love does not ask that question, not while you live as one flesh with your spouse. You are one flesh: one man, one woman, for one lifetime – your spouse's lifetime or yours – until death do you part. Death: that brings us to the third guiding star.

Discussion Questions for Chapter Two:
The Doctrine of Creation Directs Our Journey Into Intimacy

1. What is meant by "creation needs?"

2. What were the three foundational "creation needs" which God met during creation week?

3. What "creation need" was met by the creation of Adam?

4. What "creation need" was met by the creation of the woman?

5. What is signified by God's act of bringing the woman to Adam and Adam's act of naming her?

6. Why is the question "Could I be married to someone else?" "a denial of divine providence and an insult to love?"

3

The Doctrine of The Fall Directs our Journey into Marital Intimacy

THE ESSENCE OF DEATH IS SEPARATION

Genesis 3 records man's fall, through sin, into death. Although we live immersed in death, few understand death biblically. Death is not annihilation. Death is not oblivion. Death is not evaporation into nothingness. Death is not nonexistence. Biblically defined, the essence of death is precisely as the old marriage vow says, "till death do us part." Death is a parting, a separation, a division. Death rips the unities of created life apart. Death sunders life's interconnections. God joined all creation together into a unified, living whole. What God joins, death separates. Death rips everything out of its place. Death disconnects, and destroys the order that God originally established in creation. If you would understand death biblically, you must think of death as a separation, a division, a rending asunder.

Satan, the liar and the murderer, was able to intrude into the living intimacy of the first couple and instigate their severance from themselves, from creation, and even from God. We seldom give place to Satan in our view of life as we should. Yes, we know the "story" of the Fall, but we seldom give due weight to the role that Satan, that deceiver, plays when we think about the large issues of evil and its origin. Satan is still intent on killing us and our marriages through his lies and enticements.

Consider how death permeates our experience of this life. Death conditions fallen man's own psyche, his own sense of himself. He experiences death's separation even within himself. Adam, before the Fall, would not have thought the way we think. Our minds are fallen. We are born separated from God in spiritual death (cf. Ephesians 2.1-3). Unfallen Adam was alive. He experienced life in union with the Creator and the creation. His consciousness was thoroughly other-directed. He was not self-absorbed as we are. He self-consciously knew himself as image of God and as such he embraced his God, his wife, and his stewardship of the earth. It would never have dawned on him to separate himself from all of those unions. He had no reason to cut himself off from all to which God had united him and no reason to isolate himself. Unfallen man had no sense of himself except in living union with his wife, his work in the world, and his God. He would never have separated himself from those living unions to be a disconnected individual, alone and isolated. He could not know himself as a solitary man. He would not try to stand outside himself and look back in on himself and say, "Hey, I'm me!"

Before the Fall, Adam would have known himself only in living unions: in union with God, with Isshah, with the earth through his labor, with the animals and the vegetation under his dominion. Nothing would impel him to disconnect himself from these unities to look at himself in an introverted, self-focused, self-centered manner. Such is the mind-set of death. Our fallen self-centeredness is itself the evidence that we are spiritually dead. We experience this fallen life with death permeating our perspective on ourselves and the world. Unless God's redeeming grace intervenes, we will live as dead men: separated disconnected, detached.

Before the Fall, Adam would not have had the same self-consciousness that we have as fallen sinners. But after he ate of that fruit, his eyes opened and he looked at the world from the vantage point of death: separated, disconnected, isolated, and alone. In Genesis 2.17, God warned the man that if he ate of the forbidden fruit, he would *surely die*. But Satan promised that if they ate, their *eyes would be opened* (Genesis 3.5). So they ate *and then the eyes of both of them were opened* (verse 7). They experienced Satan's promised "enlightenment," but God calls it "death." They ate and began to see the world through the eyes of two dead people! They opened their eyes to a world engulfed by death, a world that had begun to rip apart at the seams. Creation broke in the Fall. Before the Fall there were seamless unions. Now divisions emerged as death permeated everything.

Fig leaf rebellion

As soon as they sinned, Ish and Isshah immediately acted like two dead people: they separated from each other. Then they took fig leaves, with which they made neither earmuffs, nor sunglasses, nor party hats. They made loin coverings. They separated precisely at the point of their one-flesh intimacy. Physical intimacy gives expression to a full-orbed heart and soul intimacy. By their sin, they killed their intimacy, they murdered their union and intimacy's epitome expression was buried beneath a leaf.

The couple now is a broken image of God. You look at

them, but they present a disfigured picture of God. You no longer see a picture of plurality in unity. You see separation, isolation, severance: death. The picture of primal perfection presented in Genesis 2.24-25 is now twisted and distorted. In that picture, you see a naked, unashamed couple bound in seamless intimacy and properly placed in context of an ordered creation. Now they have loin coverings, separated in shame from each other, and disconnected from all that God had joined them in the original creation.

The fig-leaf represents an extensive rebellion. For one thing, it announced death's separation between mankind and the earth, between mankind and the plants. God had given the plants to them for food, to be life-giving to them. The couple was to cultivate and keep the earth. But the fig-leaf was a rejection of God's order and purpose. The fig-leaf declared that man no longer accepted stewardship of the earth to cultivate and to keep it. They now used the plants which God had given to them for food to rebel against God Himself.

For another thing, the fig-leaf announced the couple's rejection of God's purposes for themselves. God told them to be fruitful and multiply. But they rejected God's purpose. They cannot fulfill this part of the dominion mandate with loin coverings on. They took a plant, ripped it up and used it to pry each other apart. In effect, they got a divorce. They turned away from each other and away from God's design for them in marriage.

The fig-leaf was also a weapon used against God, a barricade to keep God away. When God came to walk in the cool of the day, the two of them ran and hid behind trees. They used creation to fend off their Creator-Father. God gave them those trees as material they were to use for His glory. But they used the trees to build a barricade to keep God away from them, to oppose Him.

Originally, the Lord was God over the man who, in union with the woman, exercised dominion over the animals and plants in a creation without Satan. Now, everything is now out of order, inside out and upside down. Satan has commandeered an animal and used a tree to deceive the woman and pull her out of her place of union with the man, who has now believed the lie that he can become divine and live in a creation without God. The pieces have fallen apart and lie broken in bits. It is grievous and embarrassing. I can picture Adam cowering behind a bush, and the woman crouched behind another bush. The two of them are separated and hardly even looking at each other. In total self-absorption, they vainly try to hide from the omniscient God who is their Creator, Father, and Judge. We look at them in their fig leaf rebellion, and we see ourselves.

Divine justice

God arraigned the three criminals and began to question the one primarily responsible: Adam. Listen to our first father in Genesis 3.12. *And the man said, "The woman whom You gave to be with me, she gave me from the tree, and I ate."* We might be inclined to pity Adam and say, "Aw, poor Adam. He's being victimized. He was preyed on by that conniving serpent that came out of nowhere and took advantage of him! Poor guy!" True, we need to factor Satan into our understanding of sin and the Fall far more than we usually do. But we cannot minimize the wickedness of Adam's sin. Do you see what he does? In verse 12, *the man said* – now, watch his arms, can you see his arms? *The woman You* (one arm extends pointing a finger at God) *gave to me, she* (the other arm extends a pointing finger at Isshah) *made me eat*.

The woman you gave to me. We call this blame-shifting. Adam in effect seeks divorce. He separates from her and stands before the authorities and says, "I am not going to take responsibility for her any more. She is not my wife; she is 'the woman,' that thing over there." Adam is dead to her, and would see her dead. "Do You have a death sentence to carry out, God? *The woman!* If someone must die, execute her. And by the way, *You* gave her to me. So, You are the One who is to blame for all of this!"

This is bold, willful wickedness. Adam has fallen deeply into death. He not only separated from God and God's purposes, he stands in defiant rebellion against God, wickedly charging God with blame for the sin which he committed. Limply, Adam's deflated admission, *and I ate,* trails behind his blame-shifting evasions. Isshah made the same afterthought admission, except that she was right to expose the serpent as the deceiver – something Adam did not do. Adam had aligned himself more with Satan than with God. Judicially, God would have been righteous had He cast the two of them with Satan and his fallen angels into the lake of fire, right then and there. They have shown themselves more desirous to be spiritually intimate with Satan than with God. They would rather trust Satan's lying words than God's words of truth. They would rather believe that they can sin and escape punishment, than that they will surely die. They have tried to make gods of themselves and have trusted in lies. The only explanation for their knowledge of being naked and their fig-leaf separation of death is their sin. Their admission of guilt, although meager, nevertheless demands unmitigated judgment.

Divine grace

But God came into the garden and called the fallen couple, not to damn them, but to save them. God came and revealed Himself to be gracious. He salvaged creation and He retained both the man and the woman in their respective roles according to His original design. But death has come, as God said it would. We must never deceive ourselves. Whatever a man sows, that is what he shall reap. Man ate the fruit and disobeyed, and *the wages of sin is death – but the free gift of God is eternal life in Christ Jesus our Lord* (Romans 6:23). Free grace comes to fallen mankind who stands guilty in sin, fallen into death, deceived by Satan.

In Genesis 3.15,16 we read God's words of grace to Isshah:

> *I will put enmity between you and the woman and between your seed and her seed. He shall bruise you on the head and you shall bruise Him on the heel. To the woman, He said, 'I will greatly multiply your pain in childbirth. In pain you shall bring forth children, yet your desire shall be for your husband and he shall rule over you.*

God intervened. God came to salvage creation from death and to save sinners from the judgment that sin deserves. Despite the woman's alignment with Satan, God put hostility between them and broke up their alliance. The woman would not align herself with Satan but would continue in alignment with the man. As the Primal Preacher, God Himself prophesied of the coming Savior to Satan in the hearing of the couple. God salvaged the man and the woman, kept them in their original roles, and announced the gospel to fallen mankind. The woman would continue in her role as wife and mother. Likewise the man would continue to be the laborer and the namer.

Yet death would condition the man's experience of labor as well as the woman's experience of childbirth. The man will continue to labor as God originally intended, but his labor will be full of pain and frustration. The woman will continue to be a mother as God originally intended, but her labor will be full of pain and frustration. The Lord used the same word to describe the pain that a woman experiences in childbearing and the frustration a man experiences in his work. When a woman is giving birth she undergoes a contraction. The pain intensifies and then passes and what does she have for all her strain and stress? She has the opportunity to have another contraction. Along comes another contraction, and what do she have? More contractions! In a less intense and more protracted way, the man experiences a similar painful frustration in his work as that experienced more intensely by a woman in labor. What does he have for all his effort and strain? He has an opportunity for another contraction. The woman experiences *pain* and the man experiences *toil*. Those are English translations of the same Hebrew word. He experiences the pain of toiling only to harvest thorns and thistles. She experiences the pain of straining through a contraction only to give birth to nothing. Frustration now conditions our experience in this fallen world.

Although we are fallen and groan under the burden of death, God has preserved us as males and females with our original identities and roles. After the Fall, Adam was still the namer. In Genesis3.20 he called his wife's name, *Eve*. He changed her name from Isshah to Eve: the mother of all the living. He believed God's promise that the woman would give birth to the One who would crush the head of the serpent. So he renamed Isshah with hope in the Promised One who will triumph over Satan and bring life - life without death - to earth once again. Through Eve there will come the One who will bring life and undo the work of the Devil. In Genesis 3.21, the Lord ministered to the couple as undeserving sinners. He shed the blood of another *living creature* to cover the couple's consciousness of sin. God's act of making garments for the fallen couple is the door through which the history of blood atonement opens up, pointing to that full and final atonement made for sin through the shedding of the blood of Jesus. The fallen couple was expelled from the garden, that primal temple of God, until the seed would come, atonement be made, and the head of the serpent crushed. Then, in Christ Jesus, men would be given access to the tree of life and enter into God's eternal Sabbath rest. Will we see Adam in heaven? I believe so, because he renamed the woman in the hope of salvation. He was a fallen sinner who believed God's promise about the promised seed, Jesus Christ. All in heaven are precisely that: fallen sinners who believe in God's gracious salvation given to us in Jesus Christ.

A PROPENSITY TO PERVERSION

Moses has all along presented Isshah as Adam's wife. Before the Fall, Ish and Isshah were married (Genesis 2.25) and the man exercised "headship" (Genesis 2.23). During the Fall, the couple are presents as married (Genesis 3.6, 8) and the man held responsible as the "head" (Genesis 3.9). After the Fall, Moses still describes them as *husband and wife*, in spite of their "fig-leaf divorce" (Genesis 3.16, 17, 20, 21) and the punishment of death is leveled through the man as the legal representative (Genesis 3.19) who yet exercises headship by naming the woman *Eve* (Genesis 3.20). In spite of the lies, rebellion and death, God's purposes for creation are intact. But creation has indeed fallen into death through sin, and marriage itself is now visited with the sentence of death which threatens to kill the intimacy God designed for His image-bearers.

Genesis 3.16 reads, *Yet your desire shall be for your husband, and he shall rule over you*. Genesis 4.7 reads, *sin is crouching at the door; and its desire is for you, but you must master it*. When we compare these verses we see the same Hebrew vocabulary and grammatical construction. In Genesis 3.16, Moses is describing an inherent post-Fall tension in marriage. Although God salvaged marriage in Genesis 3.16, and although the original gender roles continue, a form of death has come upon marriage itself. Marriage now knows its own unique 'pain' and frustration. The sexes now contend with the threat of death, with the inclination to separate, to move away from oneness into division, even into conflict. The point of the frustration and conflict is over the issue of leadership, or headship. This is the issue that threatens to divide and separate us as married couples: who is going to lead in the marriage?

God established Adam's headship before He created the woman. Some students of Scripture only trace the beginnings of male headship back to the Fall and view it as a punishment inflicted on the woman. Male headship is not a divine punishment visited on the woman. God designed godly male headship in creation to be a blessing for the woman. Adam exercised such a headship by naming and ruling. When God brought the woman to him, he instinctively exercised leadership. He identified her in union with himself and assumed responsibility to nurture and provide for her. He expressed his leadership by communicating words that gave meaning and significance to life. Adam's pre-Fall words accurately aligned with the revealed words of God. But Satan attacked the man in his position of headship and his possession of God's words. He isolated the woman and questioned God's words. The man was steward of both the woman and God's words and, in graciously salvaged world he continued to have those stewardships. But the salvaged world was still a fallen world. God reunited the couple, but their marriage was fragile, vulnerable, and subject to death and sin.

Today we live in a world created by God, conditioned by death, but salvaged in grace. God still gives us the creation ordinance of marriage but, in this fallen world, we can easily abuse marriage. Two sinners, susceptible to their respective sins, marry. Because of their sin, the couple contends with the influence of death that threatens to separate them. To the degree that they tolerate separation, not intimacy, their marriage presents a distorted picture of the plurality-in-unity being of God. The point at which marriage is most vulnerable concerns the question of headship. When unbiblical leadership is exercised in marriage, the marriage is perverted and twisted into something deformed. It is at the point of leadership that marriage has a propensity to perversion.

On the one hand, there is what I call 'the perversion of extremes.' In this deformity of marriage, the man takes his headship to an extreme and the woman takes her submission to an extreme. He twists his headship into tyranny and she submits herself to the point of effacement. His rule is everything and she is nothing. He perverts his masculinity and domineers, and she submits to the point of erasing her God-given femininity. You see this 'perversion of extremes' in Eastern cultures. Husbands in these cultures are often tyrants with license to dominate their wives even to the point of abuse. The husband is given excessive, extreme authority which he exercises arbitrarily, often without love or accountability. The wife assumes an extreme submission. She becomes invisible, even hidden behind a veil, without personal identity.

On the other hand, you can twist marriage in the opposite direction and have what I call 'the perversion of inversion.' Now the husband abdicates his headship and the wife usurps the headship. This is the dominant marital deformity of Western cultures. When we invert the roles of husband and wife, the marriage looks more like a mother parenting her son. When the wife assumes domestic authority, she naturally exercises that authority as a mother. She leads her immature husband like a mother guiding and protecting her son. He gets her permission for his boyish indulgences and she gets the right to rule. They seem to have a workable arrangement, but eventually the matriarchy breeds contempt. She comes to resent being married to a boy, not a man. He comes to resent her for not treating him as the man he is yet to become.

When we pervert God-defined gender roles, we bring death to marriage, death to intimacy, and death to the glory of God in our marriages. Such marital deformity is sin, and sin obstructs intimacy. Sin must be overcome with gospel love, which brings us to our fourth and final guiding star.

Discussion Questions for Chapter Three: The Doctrine of the Fall Directs Our Journey Into Marital Intimacy

1. What is the essential meaning of "death"?

2. How did death affect Adam's self-consciousness?

3. What is Satan's "enlightenment"?

4. How did the Fall "present a disfigured picture of God?"

5. What are the three ways in which the fig leaf symbolized death for the couple?

6. What one word sums up Adam's response to God's questions?

7. Rather than damning the couple, how does God respond to their sin?

8. How is death visited on the couple?

9. Will we see Adam in heaven? Why?

10. In this fallen world, what is the point of frustration and conflict in marriage?

11. What is meant by "the perversion of extremes"?

12. What is meant by "the perversion of inversion"?

4

The Doctrine of Redemption Directs our Journey into Marital Intimacy

A Showcase For The Gospel

In Ephesians 5.22-33 we read:

> *Wives, be subject to your own husbands, as to the Lord. For the husband is the head of the wife, as Christ also is the head of the church, He Himself being the Savior of the body. But as the church is subject to Christ, so also the wives ought to be to their husbands in everything. Husbands, love your wives, just as Christ also loved the church and gave Himself up for her; that He might sanctify her, having cleansed her by the washing of water with the word, that He might present to Himself the church in all her glory, having no spot or wrinkle or any such thing; but that she should be holy and blameless. So husbands ought also to love their own wives as their own bodies. He who loves his own wife loves himself; for no one ever hated his own flesh, but nourishes and cherishes it, just as Christ also does the church, because we are members of His body. For this cause a man shall leave his father and mother, and shall cleave to his wife; and the two shall become one flesh.*

> *This mystery is great; but I am speaking with reference to Christ and the church. Nevertheless let each individual among you also love his own wife even as himself; and let the wife see to it that she respect her husband.*

We need to define our marriages according to the gospel. We need to understand that our marriages portray Christ's marriage to His church. We need to display "gospel love" in our marriages and orient our marriages toward redemptive purposes. We see redemptive love in Christ's love for His Bride. He loves her, so He gave Himself for her. He purposes to sanctify His bride, to wash her with the Word, and to present her to Himself in holiness and purity. What does this love look like? The apostle of New Covenant grace points us to the picture of the first couple, before the Fall, in one-flesh unity in a world of perfect order. In Ephesians 5.31 he argues for Christian marriage from Genesis 2.24. We look back at Genesis 2 and in so doing peer into the future! We look back to the beginning and we see a depiction of the redeemed church, the bride of Christ, who will be united to the last Adam in sinless unity. We look at Genesis 2 and we see what God has purposed for His people in the culmination of redemption. We look at the beginning and we see the end. We see that God created with a redemptive purpose. Paul tells us that *God, who created all things* did so *in accordance with the eternal purpose which He carried our in Christ Jesus our Lord* (Ephesians 3.9,10). God's eternal purpose of redemption is revealed in the culminating scene of creation. The sinless couple in loving intimacy is a picture of Christ and His redeemed church. Paul says, *This mystery is great*. It is this mystery that we, as Christians, are to depict in our marriages.

A SIGNPOST TO GLORY

A gospel-defined, godly marriage is a marriage defined according to God's original pre-Fall design, a design that He salvaged out of the Fall, a design which has redemptive significance. When two Christians marry, they obey God's will revealed in the creation ordinance of marriage, but they elevate marriage by giving it new creation significance. They fill marriage with the life of the resurrected Jesus Christ by the power of the Holy Spirit. Their love is given to them by God in Christ, and defined in terms of the gospel. They then learn to give each other this "gospel love" and through the gospel, they are enabled by the Spirit to overcome those sins that threaten marital intimacy.

With gospel love we, as a married couple, look at Genesis 2.24 and see our future salvation. Our marriages become a means to glorify our Creator and our Redeemer. Our marriages display both the order of creation and the hope of salvation. Our marriages refract the light of creation and point to the coming glory of our Lord Jesus Christ through whom we have been created and by whom we are redeemed. As we align our marriages with God's original purposes, we do so through the power and life of the resurrected Lord. By loving each other with gospel love, we display the triumph of Christ over sin and death, and we "prophesy" of the coming age.

A Christian marriage points to the coming of Christ for His Bride, the church which John sees in Revelation 21.1-3:

> *And I saw a new heaven and a new earth; for the first heaven and the first earth passed away, and there was no longer any sea. And I saw the holy city, New Jerusalem, coming down out of heaven from God, made ready as a*

> *bride adorned for her husband. And I heard a loud voice from the throne, saying, "Behold, the tabernacle of God is among men, and He shall dwell among them, and they shall be His peoples, and God Himself shall be among them.*

The bride is presented, covenant intimacy is consummated, and eternal sinless union with the God who indwells His people commences.

Marriages of covenant fidelity and gospel intimacy are signposts to glory. When we align our marriages with God's original ordinance we point to the glory of our Creator. When we clothe our marriages with gospel love we point to the glorious grace that God now gives to sinners in Christ. But our marriages also point to the future, to the glory of the next age. Christian marriage stands on the bedrock of creation and reflects the glory of the Triune God. Christian marriage is thoroughly conditioned by the triumph of the gospel and displays the love of God in Christ Jesus. Christian marriage points to the future consummation of Christ's love for His church. Are these not glorious purposes for marriage?

Today many psychologists, therapists, sociologists and politicians attempt to commandeer marriage and urge us to approach marriage from a man-centered perspective. Let us view marriage as true theologians, as students of Scripture, with a God-centered perspective. Let us concern ourselves with the glory of God in our marriage. It is only as we learn to live for the glory of God and not for ourselves, that we will discover our own nobility and purpose. Glorify God in your marriage and experience the dignity of being the image of God, and the redeemed of the Lord!

Take your wife's hand, brother. Grasp his hand firmly, sister. Stand together as the apex of creation. Together, you are the astonishing image of God. Put your feet on the bedrock of Genesis 2.24. Stand united in Christ. What nobility and God-glorifying dignity is yours as you endeavor, more and more, to become one flesh! Together you can demonstrate how the gospel triumphs over sin and death. Together you can be a signpost, pointing all who know you to the hope that is ours in the coming of Christ and the glories of the new heavens and earth.

Navigate your marriage by these four guiding stars. Glorify God, live in the reality of God's creation, conquer sin and display the gospel with the resurrection power of the age to come. Here is a journey worth taking – the journey into marital intimacy.

Discussion Questions for Chapter Four:
The Doctrine of Redemption Directs Our Journey Into Intimacy

1. How do the doctrine of creation and the gospel inform a Christian couple's marriage?

2. How does a Christian marriage become "a signpost to glory"?

3. Sum up how "the four guiding stars" direct us into marital intimacy.

PART TWO:

MARITAL INTIMACY AND THE GRACE OF GOSPEL LOVE

Introduction

The classic World War II love song stayed on the pop-charts for decades, probably because it expressed a timeless truth. "You Always Hurt The One You Love" was written in 1944 by Allan Roberts and Doris Fisher. The lyrics are as follows:

> You always hurt the one you love
> The one you shouldn't hurt at all.
> You always take the sweetest rose
> And crush it till the petals fall;
> You always break the kindest heart
> With a hasty word you can't recall;
> So if I broke your heart last night,
> It's because I love you most of all.

Sometimes when we try to love someone, our efforts backfire. Rather than pleasing them, we hurt them. Why is it so hard for us to love? It is so hard for us to love because we are sinners, and even as Christians, we still contend with our sin which erupts and we end up hurting the one we love. There is only one solution to the problem of our sin: the gospel. If we are going to develop true intimacy, we are going to have to learn how to overcome our sin. If we are going to develop true intimacy, we are going to have to learn how to love each other with "gospel love." Gospel love is the practical application of the gospel to the sin that, if left unresolved, will hurt the one you love, and will hurt you, and bring dishonor to Christ.

5

The Challenge of Gospel Love

The intimacy we need: "Love me"

We respond to the prospect of marital intimacy with some ambivalence.

We experience both an attraction and an aversion to the prospect of intimacy.

Intimacy attracts us because God made us for intimacy. God made us to be intimate with Him. God made us to be intimate with our spouse. When we were married, we became one flesh. By our one-flesh union, we are to image the divine intimacy which the persons of the Triune Godhead enjoy. The intimacy known by God's two-in-one creatures is a reflection of the being of, and intimacy known by the God who is Three-in-One, a plurality in unity. As His image bearers, we are oriented toward and attracted to intimacy.

Adam, before the Fall, did not have an individualized self-consciousness like our fallen self-consciousness. He would not have defined himself as detached and isolated from his God, his wife, his labor and his creation stewardships. He would not have understood himself with a severed self-consciousness conditioned by death. But his fall through sin into death brought this experience of division into and within himself. As a fallen sinner, he not only separated himself from God and creation, but he experienced separation within himself. Before the Fall, he would not have thought about himself as disconnected from the creation into which God had intimately knit him. He would not have studied his 'self' as we, in our fallen state, are so prone to do. He would not have known himself in any other context than that of his union with God, the earth, his labor, God's words, the animals, the plants, and his wife. Adam would have had no knowledge of himself other than that which God revealed to him by having created him in His image and having assigned the creation mandate to him.

After the Fall, God salvaged creation and preserved the man and the woman in their original place. So even though we are fallen, we still live according to the original order of God's creation. By nature we bear God's image as God originally designed: imaging Him in our labor, our family, and ourreligion. We instinctively seek intimacy and join ourselves to those endeavors and those people with whom we find significance and fulfillment. When we ponder the prospect of marital intimacy, it attracts us.

We yearn for someone to know us, to understand us, and to accept us. This desire to be understood propels us to seek intimacy with others. We long for companionship. We are social beings by nature. *It is not good for the man to be alone* (Genesis 2.18). Loneliness is an unbearable pain from which we seek relief, if not in personal engagement with another person, then with a pet. If another person or pet is not available, we will personalize an inanimate object, like the Tom Hanks character Chuck Noland in the 2000 film version of Robinson Crusoe, *Castaway*. Chuck Noland has to talk to someone. Robinson Crusoe talked to God, Chuck talks to his volleyball: Wilson. Chuck has to talk to someone because he is a social being. He needs personal intimacy even if it is with his own bloody handprint smeared on a volleyball. We watch Chuck talking passionately to his volleyball, and we understand. We know why he is doing that. He needs intimacy. He wants to be loved, even if only by projecting himself back onto himself off his volleyball.

The privacy we want: "Leave me alone"

Modern man, although made for intimacy, wants privacy. That is our modern demand: the right of privacy. Modern man wants the right to hide behind his fig leaf. He wants to be able to be alone in the darkness of his self-indulgences where, ironically, he often seeks the specter of intimacy without the legitimate demands of intimacy. He spends hours as a disembodied persona in an internet chat room where he hides behind his pseudonym seeking a perverse intimacy: an intimacy without physical presence. Cyber-souls sit in the steamy sauna of internet chat, unzipping their hearts, expressing their secrets to disembodied entities that may or may not be who they say they are. Internet pornography offers the same angst-ridden attraction: the chance to stay hidden while becoming intimate with what is most private. Modern man is attracted to the prospect of sex without intimacy. He wants to be loved, but has hidden himself beneath the fig leaves of superficial social roles and self-deception.

With our cherished right of privacy we live disconnected lives in a fragmented society. The modern technological lifestyle affects even how we live out our faith. For example, what does "local" mean when we speak of "the local church?" The local church is not local today the way it used to be. We live in one county, we work in another county, we go to church in another county, and our children go to school in another county or even another state. Our extended family lives in another state or even another country. We navigate among the islands where we perform our various tasks and relate to various clusters of people. As we move from island to island, we are liable to become socially schizophrenic, having one persona on one island and another persona on another island. We can become a certain character at work, a different character at church, and yet another character in the home. All the while we can be reasonably confident that none of these social environments will ever overlap one another. We can lose track of ourselves as we don various costumes and play-act different roles on several stages each with their own supporting casts. Amid such social fragmentation, our associations with others become superficial, sporadic, unengaged, and distant.

Intimacy attracts us, but - because of our sin - we are also averse to the prospect of intimacy. Although God made us for intimacy, we sinfully separate ourselves from others. We still stitch fig leaves together and run away hurting, hiding, wanting someone to find us. Privately, we still want intimacy, but our sin drives us into isolated self-absorption. There, alone with self, we are reminded of things we want to keep hidden. Intimacy involves exposure. Intimacy invades privacy. But we know our shame. We know our sin. So we cover ourselves with any convenient fig leaf. When intimacy approaches, we start maneuvering; dodging, weaving, and avoiding direct contact in case we disclose our true selves. We evade, deceive, and lie. Lies keep people away, at a distance, not up close and intimate.

We strangely strive to be private and hidden even to our selves. Lies not only stifle intimacy with others, they hinder our ability to be intimate even with ourselves. The person we are most likely to deceive is our self. Scripture repeatedly warns us against self-deception.[6] Due to sin, we can not only live deceptively detached from others, but self-deceived and unknown even to our selves. We do not even want intimacy with our selves!

Marital intimacy has a way of breaking through the layers of self-deception. It was common when I was young for people to go off on some journey to a distant land to "find oneself." Actually, self-discovery is more often found in the journey into marital intimacy. Finding myself was one of my most unsettling discoveries during the early years of my marriage. Getting to know my wife was a privilege, but what I learned about myself was painful. I was not the loving, caring, romantic guy I thought I was in my singleness. I had deceived myself. But I yearned for intimacy. I needed intimacy in the innermost core of my being. Yet the prospect of being intimate repelled me because the closer I got to my wife, the more I discovered my sin and less often, my wife's sin. The eruptions of sin hurt us. The pain of our sin made us pull back from each other. It brought death and threatened to separate us. Learning to be intimate was painful, but I knew that, for me, being single was more painful. I knew that it was not good for this man to be alone. Thankfully, I wanted intimacy more than I wanted to continue in my self-centered self-absorption. I started to stop kidding myself and, by the grace of God, forced myself to get honest and be honest with God and with my wife. I had discovered that deception murders intimacy.

We often purchase the culturally valued commodity of privacy with the currency of deception. But the reality of who we are as created in the image of God compels us to be counter-cultural and to reach out for intimacy, even marital intimacy. So we marry. Marriage summons us to love and love demands honesty and honesty relinquishes privacy. When we marry, our privacy evaporates.

The invading conscience

Our longing for someone to know and understand us draws us into marriage. But when we marry, we immediately feel like we have been invaded and intruded upon. We want to be known but becoming intimate is disturbing. There is no privacy in marriage. She is everywhere I am. She is in my bedroom. He is in my bathroom. She is in my living room. He is in my car. She identifies, classifies, and tags my self-conscious and unselfconscious habits and puts them on display before me like unearthed artifacts in a museum. I was quite comfortable with that habit, I never even knew I had that attitude, and now, there I am, exposed under the light of not one, but two consciences! My private habits and moods are now scrutinized and morally assessed in the public presence of this "invader" who compels me to take responsibility for things I had tucked neatly beneath my fig leaf. This is what is so unsettling about intimacy: it is the constant presence of another conscience. It is the constant presence of another judge who insists on evaluating the minutiae of my life.

Judgment: that is the problem with intimacy. Intimacy often feels like judgment and judgment is precisely what I, in my sin, would flee. Sinners spontaneously run from the prospect of being judged. God comes in the cool of the day:

the divine conscience arrives and I swiftly depart! I go behind a tree and start pointing and blaming someone else, trying to divert God's gaze away from my privacy. Marriage can feel like judgment. Here comes another conscience and there goes my privacy. She invades my otherwise detached privacy and shines the light of her conscience beneath my social superficiality and it feels like judgment. I am tempted to hide from her. What she learns about me makes me uncomfortable. She invades me. But I want her to know me, to love me, to accept me. I want intimacy, but it is expensive. The cost of intimacy is the willingness to be judged. That is what it costs to be intimate. If we would experience intimacy, we must pay the price of having our privacy exposed and judged. Intimacy challenges us and asks, "Is your love deeper than that ingrained sin? Is your love stronger than that unbreakable habit? Can your love spur you on to overcome that character flaw that you would otherwise carry to your grave?" This is expensive. This is dangerous. Will I choose my cherished indulgences, my cultivated flaws, and my sin instead of my wife, instead of my husband? These are anguishing choices. Have I not repeatedly chosen my sin? Have I not proven that I am able to destroy friendships, offend intimates, and separate from others and isolate myself? But I know that it is not good for me to be alone. I want intimacy. I am made for intimacy. I need intimacy. Yet when I reach out to be intimate, my sin erupts and threatens to kill intimacy.

The love that overcomes sin

Here is the real issue in all this privacy stuff: we do not want our spouse to expose our sin. That is the trouble with being intimate. It brings us a fresh discovery of our sin. We find ourselves as the disciples when they said to Jesus in Matthew 19.10, *If the relationship of a man and his wife is like this, it is better not to marry*. What compels us to seek intimacy when so much within us opposes intimacy? Why choose intimacy when it costs us our privacy, when it exposes our cherished self-indulgences and renders us constantly liable to being judged? Why be intimate only to see your deep-rooted heart sins continually being dredged up into the light of mutual scrutiny? Why be intimate only to be repeatedly painfully reminded of things you wish could stay hidden? Why pay this price? And yet how can you be human, much less married, and not want intimacy?

What does Christ give us to enable us to overcome our sinful reluctance to be intimate while satisfying our inherent hunger to be intimate? Love. *Above all, keep fervent in your love for one another, because love covers a multitude of sin* (1 Peter 4.8). Love. Only love can overcome the sin that threatens to kill intimacy.

No doubt most, if not all, married couples would say that they married because they "fell in love." Love is the explanation we give for marriage. Remember all the objections that our friends hurled against us when we announced our wedding plans?They barraged us with objections, and demanded an answer to the question "Why?" Why did we decide to marry? Well, because we were confident that we were in love. What about those of us who are in our middle years, watching the odometer pass through cycles of decades? What motivates us to overcome the challenges to intimacy? What will keep us on the course mapped out by the four guiding stars?

What will enable us to withstand the threatened mutinies, the careless dereliction of duty? What will keep the rudder firm against the waves, the crosscurrents, and the gale force winds of certain crisis? What will keep us going amid the foggy, motionless stillness of lulls in our love? What will keep us on course is what I am calling "gospel love."

Discussion Questions for Chapter Five:
The Challenge To Gospel Love

1. Why is it so hard for us to love someone with out hurting them in the process

2. Why are we attracted to intimacy?

3. How did Adam experience the divisions that his fall into death brought

4. What about marriage attracts us?

5. What is the so-called "right" of modern man which poses a threat to intimacy

6. How has the internet provided opportunities for "a perverse intimacy?"

7. How does our modern commuting lifestyle threaten intimacy?

8. Why does the prospect of intimacy appear threatening to us?

9. From whom do we often try to hide?

10. What does love demand that will require us to relinquish our privacy?

11. "Marriage can feel like judgment." Why?

12. What is "the cost of intimacy?"

13. What are the choices intimacy demands of us?

14. What does Christ give us that enables us to overcome our reluctance to be intimate?

6

The Enemy of Gospel Love

NOT ANY OLD LOVE WILL DO

Who does not esteem and value love? Who would oppose love? Who does not love love? Culture presents us with poetic panegyrics to love in our music, art, entertainment and literature. In the praise of love, we promote the noble virtues of generosity, compassionate concern, romantic affection, and stalwart faithfulness to duty. Yet, in spite of all that is done and said to extol love, true love is rare and desperately needed.

You are familiar with Paul's description of love in 1 Corinthians 13. There he tells us what love is as he describes love in action. Love is patient, and love is kind. Love humbly endures in righteousness, truth and hope. The portrait of love in 1 Corinthians 13 is set against the backdrop of the darkness of sin. The context in which we see love, the reality in which we define love, in which love proves itself, is the reality of sin. Love overcomes sin.

1 John 4.7-11 urges us to biblical love, that is, gospel love.

> *Beloved, let us love one another, for love is from God; and everyone who loves is born of God and knows God. The*

> *one who does not love does not know God, for God is love. By this the love of God was manifested in us, that God has sent His only Begotten Son into the world so that we might live through Him. In this is love, not that we loved God, but that He loved us and sent His Son to be the propitiation for our sins. Beloved, if God so loved us, we also ought to love one another.*

John defines love theologically: *God is love*. Here we have the light of our first guiding star shining on the subject. God shows love by sending His Son as the propitiation for our sins, as the sacrifice which appeased divine wrath and averted divine judgment. In the sacrificial death of Jesus we have atonement for our sin. He assumed the punishment which we rightly deserve. By His obedient self-sacrifice, He paid the penalty for our sin. By His death, He defeated death by satisfying the demands of God's justice. By His resurrection He triumphs in new life, the life of eternity, the life of love. Here then is love. Love works to promote life. Love seeks to solve the problem of death caused by sin. Love mends sin's separations. Love brings life and unity. Sin brings death. Only gospel love can overcome sin and bring life to what would otherwise die. This is the love we are to give to each other in marriage. We are to love each other with the love that God has for us in Christ. John holds God's gospel love before us and appeals to us to love each other in the same manner as God loves us. Love each other with a love that addresses sin, that overcomes death, and that unifies what sin would otherwise separate. Take the love that God has given to you in the gospel of Jesus Christ and give that same love to each other.

This is why I am using the phrase "gospel love." It is a

love that originates in God and is expressed and defined by the gospel. Gospel love is received from the Father in Christ Jesus by a living faith engendered within us by the Holy Spirit. We receive gospel love from God and then give His love, gospel love, to our spouse. We sometimes wonder whether we are capable of loving. Are we not limited by our sin, determined by our genes, conditioned by our parents, habituated by our past? *If any man is in Christ, he is a new creature; the old things passed away; behold new things have come* (2 Corinthians 5:17). We are born of the Spirit and are new men in Christ. He has liberated us in love that we might live in love.

Gospel love is not your garden variety love of which poets sing in ballads and which actors dramatize in movies. Gospel love has to do with overcoming sin, with triumphing over death. Gospel love comes through the cross of Jesus Christ. It is God's love which we bring into our marriages by faith in the gospel. Gospel love is effective through and empowered by the Holy Spirit. The Spirit enables us to love one another the way God loves us: through the death and resurrection of Jesus Christ.

The cross issues into the resurrection. Gospel love is empowered by the resurrected Christ whose Spirit teaches us now, in this present age, to relate to one another in a way that will characterize our sinless relationships in the age to come. With gospel love, we engage one another with resurrection power. We learn to treat each other the way we will in the new heavens and the new earth. By faith in Christ who is the resurrected Lord, we receive God's gospel love. By faith we lay hold of God's love and bring it into the present fallen age, into this battleground where we contend against sin and

Satan. By faith we learn to love each other with the gospel and knit the gospel into the most intimate of all human relationships: our marriage.

GOSPEL REALISM. "YES, THAT IS SIN!"

In true marital intimacy we will taste the many flavors of love: romantic love, sexual love, giddy love, dutiful love – the pain and pleasure of love. But the marital intimacy of two believers is deeper still. We would know the love of God in our marriages. We must therefore base our marriages on gospel love. We will obtain gospel love only from God through the cross of Christ. Only gospel love will conquer sin and overpower death by the triumphant force of Christ's resurrection. We would love each other, not with the love common to this age, but with that love which is of the age to come.

The greatest enemy of love, the greatest enemy to marital intimacy, is our sin. Here again we encounter a unique frustration. Yes, many are the opponents to intimacy which attack us from outside our marriage. The fallen world is no friend to biblical love. But the greatest threat to our intimacy arises from our intimacy itself. It is the threat of our own sin and the more earnestly we seek and experience intimacy, the more vulnerable we are to the threat of our sin. The more you get to know your spouse, the more you learn of their sin. As you seek intimacy, each other's sin constantly threatens to discourage and defeat your attempts to love each other intimately.

Tricia and I were newlyweds, so we attended a Bible study for young couples. The study was lead by various older Christian couples who each took a turn addressing different topics that would be of interest to marital novices. Now, Tricia and I were hitting some speed bumps in our early months of adjustment, so we were eager to learn some practical wisdom from older more experienced couples. One of the older couples spoke to us and described their marriage. It was idyllic! As they spoke, I imagined her floating about the house in a silk nightgown, singing sweetly, bringing him his evening tea. His tender love pats synchronize with her graceful dance and their voices blend in operatic harmony as the orchestra plays with mounting crescendo and the sun gently sets over the rolling hills. The depiction they gave of their marriage was attractive, the way a fairy-tale is attractive. In our house, we were experiencing crescendos not caused by sweet strings and lilting lutes. Our symphony included the pounding tympani and clashing cymbals. We were occasionally confronting one another in caustic ways. So I ventured a question: "Well, uh, do you ever fight?" "Oh, no, no, no, we never" and he described yet more idyllic scenery. "Hmm, well, how do you, you know, how do you argue? How do you express your disagreements" "Oh, we never argue. We have never disagreed." As he continued to speak, I listened to my own incredulous thoughts. Could Tricia and I learn to live without ever arguing? "OK," I thought, "I'll come at this from a different angle." So I asked, "Well, what do you do with sin? Do you ever sin against each other?" I received more evasion and idealism and I gave up on the matter. As we drove home from the study I said to my wife, "You know, something's wrong there. Something is just not real." Soon after I learned that this was that couple's second marriage, born out of their adultery that destroyed their first marriages. Lies launched their relationship and I wondered whether lies did not still characterize their relationship. I have since learned that their marriage did not endure, the wife left him and the gentleman died without her by his side. To this day, when I meet couples that tell me they never argue, I am wary. I am inclined to think that they are either not seeking intimacy with each other and are lying to themselves, or they are not seeking intimacy with me and are lying to me. The problem in our marriages is not that we occasionally argue. We expect two sinners who are living in honest intimacy to have disagreements which occasionally veer into sinful conflict. The challenge is what we do with our sin that erupts and threatens our unity. How do we overcome the division caused by sin? Are we being honest about our sin?

A few years ago I sat on the porch of a pastor friend of mine. As we were conversing, his wife of many years brought us some refreshments. Of course that interrupted our dialog and we exchanged niceties with our hostess. As she walked away from us to go back into the house, I watched the expression on my friend's face as he gazed at her disappearing form. I remembered an old song called *The Look of Love*. Well, that look "was on his face," as the song says. The man was in love, obviously, overwhelmingly, in love. So I said to him, "You love her, don't you?" He looked at me, then looked down and shook his head, and with a low voice said, "God help me, brother, I've murdered that woman in my heart so many times." Our eyes knowingly connected and we burst out laughing. That is intimacy. That is honesty. That is the realism of two sinners who are striving for intimacy. My friend is determined to have heart dealings with his wife. The more intimacy he seeks, the more he discovers the sin that yet lurks within his heart.

Yes, we love our spouses. We would sacrifice ourselves for them, even die for them. But, as we try to love them, our remaining sin can erupt in its vile wickedness. Yes, I would die for Tricia, but, I am ashamed to admit it, there are times when, in my heart, I murder her. That is not easy to say, but it is true. I know exactly what my friend is talking about. I have experienced what Adam did when he sought to divert the death sentence from himself onto Isshah, the woman whom he was to nourish and protect. My sin (oh, it is so ugly but it is *my* sin) moves me to do what, in my heart of hearts, I do not want to do. My sin distances me from her. In my sin I withhold her nourishment; I starve her and deprive her of the care she deserves and needs, the care I promised to give her for a lifetime. I find myself naked and exposed in my sin and hear myself saying, "The woman you gave me." Those are not the words of love. Paul says *husbands ought also to love their own wives as their own bodies. He who loves his own wife loves himself; for no one ever hated his own flesh, but nourishes and cherishes it, just as Christ also does the church, because we are members of His body* (Ephesians 5.28-30). Do I nourish her? Cherish her? When I do not, Paul says I hate her, and hatred is a form of murder. I flatter myself and try to convince myself that my occasional anger against her is justified. But James 1:19,20 informs me that I'm kidding myself. *But let everyone be quick to hear, slow to speak and slow to anger; for the anger of man does not achieve the righteousness of God*. More often than not, my anger does not achieve the righteousness of God but achieves the sinful moral equivalent of murder (cf. Matthew 5:21,22).

Do you see how unsettling the pursuit of intimacy is? I want intimacy. I want to love and be loved, but I discover sin. I'm challenged then to be scripturally honest about my sin. If I am not seeking to nourish and cherish my wife, I'm not seeking her life. If I'm not seeking her life, Paul says that is equivalent to hatred and hatred is murder. It is disturbing. I try to love and in the process discover that I'm guilty of heart-murder. *Wretched man that I am!* (Romans 7:24)

The more we pursue intimacy and dig down into each other's hearts, the more we uncover ourselves and come to know of each other. We resolve to do this spade work and dig into each other because we long for intimate love. We long to be known, to be understood, and to be accepted, but we discover so much about ourselves that is unacceptable, sinful, harmful and vile. As you dig into the soil of your heart you hit this underground spring that bursts open and spews this black, acidic, clinging bile of sin on you and on your wife. It fouls the atmosphere, burns your souls and you, in your own strength, cannot get it off yourselves.

There is only one cleanser that has the strength to clean up that mess: gospel love. Only gospel love has the power to clean your life and marriage. It alone has the power to dry up that underground sewer of foulness that yet flows within your heart. Only God, who is love, can teach us to love each other. We would learn to love each other, not with a love that originates within us, but with a love that originates in God: the love that God gives us through Christ. God has given us, in union with the resurrected Christ, a supernatural, Spirit-wrought ability to love each other with God's love, a love that overcomes sin and triumphs over death.

Discussion Questions for Chapter Six:
The Enemy of Gospel Love

1. How would you distinguish "gospel love" from the kind of love that is often portrayed in culture?

2. What is "the greatest enemy to marital intimacy" and where is this threat discovered?

3. Is it right to be apprehensive of couples who say that they never argue? What is your reaction to a pastor who confesses that he has known murder in his heart toward his wife?

4. How is withholding nurture and neglecting to cherish our wives (Eph 5.28-30) a form of murder?

5. Why do we need to love each other with God's gospel love rather than the love that otherwise originates from within ourselves?

7

Be a Gospel Lover

THE LOVED LOVER

To see our identity as a 'gospel lover,' one who loves with gospel love, we will simply consider two parallel passages in Ephesians and Colossians.

> *Let all bitterness and wrath and anger and clamor and slander be put away from you, along with all malice. And be kind to one another, tenderhearted, forgiving each other, just as God in Christ also has forgiven you. Therefore, be imitators of God as beloved children; and walk in love just as Christ also loved you, and gave Himself up for us, an offering and a sacrifice to God as a fragrant aroma.*
>
> (Ephesians 4.31-5:2)

> *And so, as those who have been chosen of God, holy and beloved, put on a heart of compassion, kindness, humility, gentleness and patience; bearing with one another and forgiving each other, whoever has a complaint against anyone. Just as the Lord forgave you, so also should you. Beyond all these things, put on love, which is the perfect bond of unity.*
>
> (Colossians 3.12-14)

As Christians, we are to be gospel lovers. If we would see the triumph of gospel love in our marriages, we must firmly define ourselves as those who are in Christ, chosen of God, holy and beloved. We need to understand that, as Christians, in union with Christ and indwelt by the Spirit, we have the capacity and the equipment to love.

Love with love

How can we be confident of our ability to be gospel lovers? Is it because of our gene pool? No. Is it because our parents were such model examples for us? No. Is it because of our schooling or our education or the influence of our culture? No. We are not confident that we are gospel lovers because of any natural capacity or what we have learned from mere men.

We have the capacity to love because God has regenerated us and given new life to us. The Spirit indwells us and makes us to be partakers of the divine nature (2 Peter 1.4). We have received the gift of the Holy Spirit by whose power we can believe and apply God's gospel to our marriages. We are the chosen of God, the beloved of God, holy and sanctified in Christ Jesus. We are the temple of the Spirit. We are new creations in Christ. Old things have passed away and behold, look at it, see it, and define yourself by it, all things have become new (2 Corinthians 5.17).

You are a gospel lover only because you are loved by God with gospel love. You are loved by your heavenly Father. You are loved by the God who is love, the God who even now indwells you. He enables you to love your spouse with the love with which you are loved. To love with gospel love is simply to take the love that God has given to you in Christ and then give that love to your spouse. *Be imitators of God as beloved children. Walk in love just as Christ also loved you* (Ephesians 5.1-2). As a Christian, you are loved. Therefore, you have the capacity, the equipment and the wherewithal to love others, especially your spouse.

A DISPOSITION OF FORGIVENESS

If we would defeat our sin, the enemy of intimacy, we must learn to be gospel lovers. We must cultivate certain habits of heart. What is the essential disposition of heart which characterizes a gospel lover? Forgiveness: the willingness and faith to expect that, in union with Christ, you have the capacity to forgive sin.

Paul describes this disposition in Colossians 3.12: *Put on a heart of compassion, kindness, humility, gentleness and patience*. Likewise he says in Ephesians 4.31: *Let all bitterness and wrath and anger and clamor and slander be put away with you, along with all malice and be kind to one another, tenderhearted*. Paul describes a disposition of heart that we are to cultivate. It is a certain mind-set that you assume within yourself in keeping with your God-given identity as a gospel lover.

This is the disposition or attitude of God Himself. We read of Him in Psalm 86.5: *For Thou, Lord, art good and ready to forgive abundant in loving-kindness unto all them that call upon Thee*. God has an attitude of readiness to forgive, an inclination and bias to engage in gospel dealings. He stands ready to forgive: *the Lord longs to be gracious to you and therefore He waits on high to have compassion on you* (Isaiah 30.8).

Put on this heart of compassion, this heart of kindness, this heart of humility, gentleness and patience. Put on the heart of God who longs to be gracious, who is internally inclined to be compassionate. Have this bias, this prejudice. Have this heart orientation. Be ready and eager to apply the gospel when sin confronts you. Be ready to forgive. Be eager to deal with sin with the expectation that mercy will triumph and that grace will be victorious.

This God-like disposition is the disposition of Christ, the incarnate God. It is the disposition expressed in Jesus' prayer when He hung on the cross and cried, *Father, forgive them for they do not know what they are doing* (Luke 23.34). Jesus expressed His disposition of heart by His prayerful desire to see God's forgiveness triumph over His persecutor's sin. He exemplified His own teaching of Mark 11.25: *Whenever you stand praying, forgive, if you have anything against anyone; so that your Father also who is in heaven may forgive you your transgressions*. As He was being violated, He was praying, *Father, forgive them*. We must cultivate this disposition of gospel love in a prayerful desire to see the gospel triumph.

We will cultivate this Christ-like disposition of heart only by continual heart engagements with Jesus Christ Himself. Your spouse is not going to teach you this disposition, nor will the lyricists of popular songs. There is only One who can teach you this disposition: Christ who says, *Take My yoke upon you and learn from Me for I am gentle and humble in heart and you shall find rest for your souls* (Matthew 11.29). This is the language of discipleship. We must yoke ourselves to Jesus as His disciples and He will, by His Spirit and Word, teach us how to cultivate the disposition of gospel love. We must live in heart communion with Christ if we would learn from Him what it means to be gentle and humble of heart.

A DISPOSITION OF FORBEARANCE

If we are Christians, it is because the Spirit has united us to Jesus Christ. His Spirit empowers us to love. We must cultivate a disposition and inclination to love, and learn to forbear with each other in gospel love.

We need to cultivate a capacity to forbear: *Love covers a multitude of sins* (1 Peter 4.8). Contrary to contemporary caricatures of Christians that depict us as a most intolerant people, our Bibles teach us to be tolerant. We are patiently to endure all manner of minor offenses and not to be easily provoked or quickly offended. Our God is a God of astonishing patience. Our God is Jehovah, the God of loving-kindness, patience and forbearance. He teaches us to endure provocations. He teaches us not to tally up wrongs suffered. He teaches us that love *bears all things, believes all things, hopes all things, and endures all things* (1 Corinthians 13.7). We need to obey His instruction in our marriages. Petty annoyances, irritations and abrasions abound as we seek marital intimacy. The closer you get to your spouse, the more liable you are to petty provocations, but love *is not provoked* (1 Corinthians 13.5).

We can also say that love does not provoke. But, as you become intimate, you learn how to "push each other's buttons." You learn how to get under one another's skin and be an irritant. I have a friend who carries a little extra flesh on him. His brother likes to poke fun at him, so he used to grab his "love handles" and make a face that said, "See, look at that!" He knew how to push my friend's button and make him self-conscious. After a while, his brother could provoke him without even touching him by simply making a pinching motion with his fingers with the corresponding facial expression, and my friend knew exactly what his brother was communicating. Then it got to be where all his brother had to do was make the facial expression from across the room. He did not have to go to the trouble of walking across the room and grab my friend's flesh, or even take the trouble to motion with his hands. All he had to do was catch my friend's eye and make that facial expression. He could immediately get under his skin and provoke him. He is uniquely able to irritate his brother because he is intimate with him. They know each other well and can read each other's facial expressions in a way that no one else can.

If we want to, we can easily irritate those with whom we are intimate. We can cut right to the chase. I know the exact buzzword to use that will annoy Tricia when we discuss that sensitive topic. She knows just how to prod my raw nerve to make a poignant point. We know each other's tender spots and vulnerabilities because we are growing in our intimacy, which means we are discovering each other's weaknesses. Rather than protecting each other in view of our exposed weakness, we are tempted to provoke each other to sin. We know that just beneath the surface lies our sin, and instead of forbearing and covering sin, we can provoke and incite sin. *When sin is accomplished, it brings forth death* (James 1.15). No small part of forbearance has to do with absorbing those petty provocations and striving to allow minor annoyances to derail and distract us from the real threat to our intimacy: sin. If we spend our energy contending about how we said something, what vocabulary we used, what was meant by that voice inflection, we will not deal with the more essential issue of the sin that threatens our marital peace. Neither of us should be provocative nor easily provoked. Rather we each need to put on a disposition of forbearance; to put on a heart of kindness, gentleness and patience. *Blessed are the peacemakers, for they shall be called the sons of God* (Matthew 5.9).

Discussion Questions for Chapter Seven:
Be A Gospel Lover

1. What must we understand about ourselves if we are to be a "gospel lover?"

2. What is "the essential disposition of heart" necessary to be a gospel lover?

3. Where does this essential disposition of heart originate?

4. How does Jesus demonstrate this disposition of heart?

5. Where will we learn to cultivate this essential disposition?

6. Along with a willingness to forgive, and other disposition of heart is necessary?

7. Not only is love not provoked, but love does not provoke. How does intimacy make it easy for us to provoke our spouses and "push their buttons?"

8

The Transaction of Gospel Love

An exchange of gospel commodities

The transaction of gospel love involves two Christians. Both believers mutually reach out to each other and engage in an exchange of the gospel. Even when we cultivate the disposition of love and practice the grace of forbearance, we will still sin against our spouse. When we sin, we must mutually transact an exchange of gospel love. We must learn how to exchange gospel commodities and conduct the business of gospel love when our sin threatens our intimacy.

Here the fourth star, the doctrine of redemption, must guide us. Under the threat of sin, we must show the Christian quality of our marriage. A Christian marriage is not Christian because the couple never sins. No. What makes a marriage explicitly Christian is how the Christian couple applies the gospel when they sin. What makes the marriage Christian is the triumph of the gospel over the sin that would otherwise kill their intimacy and empty the marriage of its redemptive significance. Our marriages will not depict Christ's love for His Church unless the gospel is conquering our sin and transforming us and our marriage into Christlikeness. Gospel love is not merely something we feel or sentimentally poeticize. It is a love that takes action on the spiritual battlefield. It contends with sin and conquers death by applying the victory of the cross to the enemy of sin in the power of the resurrection.

Gospel love does the business of the gospel, and God designed the gospel to do business with our sin. When we sin, we must go to the negotiation table and take gospel commodities to transact gospel business. Have you sinned? Then it is time to transact gospel love.

Paul would have us to be *bearing with one another, forgiving each other. Whoever has a complaint against anyone, just as the Lord forgave you, so also should you* (Colossians 3.13). Paul describes an action here, not merely an attitude. We are now talking about matters in which we can no longer forbear, a *complaint* which we must address as sin and resolve through the gospel. However, if you do not have a forbearing disposition, if you do not have a gospel attitude, you will not negotiate gospel business, you will not engage in a gospel transaction.

What is the nature of this gospel transaction? It is a transaction that bridges the separation and the distance that has developed because of sin. One of you or both of you have sinned. Sin has already begun to drive a wedge between you as husband and wife. You are beginning to separate from each other and sin is threatening to kill your intimacy. Together you must face the threat of your sin. Because you are one flesh, your sin is your joint concern.

You are a Christian. You have done battle with sin before. Where and when did you learn how to overcome sin? When did you first experience the triumph of the gospel over your sin? You learned to overcome sin when *the Lord forgave you,* when you were first converted. Now, *just as the Lord forgave you, so also should you*. Do you see what the Lord did with you when He removed your sin and you became intimate with Him? Now watch how the Lord forgave you and then you and your sinning spouse act like Him, imitate your heavenly Father.

What is this gospel transaction? It is a reenactment of your conversion with your spouse. Forgive each other as the Lord forgave you. Do what He did for you when you sought Him for forgiveness. What happened in your conversion? You engaged in a gospel transaction with the Lord. You brought your confession and repentance, by faith in Christ, to God, and He gave to you the blessings of forgiveness and promised His enduring love. That is what you experienced in your conversion. Your Lord has shown you how the gospel triumphs over sin by forgiving you and becoming intimate with you. You have already been taught by God how the gospel restores intimacy. Now imitate Him and reenact your conversion with your spouse.

CONFESSION OFFERED

We must take responsibility for our sin. This is a big challenge because sin deceives, sin hardens and sin blinds, and we, like Adam in Genesis 3, are quick to shift the blame. As challenging as this is, we know that we must first be willing to discover and define our sin biblically. We have to put a biblical dipstick into the oil well of our heart, pull it out and measure it accurately. The biblical dipstick is the law of God, the Ten Commandments, and especially as that Law is fleshed out in the life, example and teachings of Jesus Christ. We need to cultivate humility and a sensitive conscience to discern and defeat the sin that threatens our intimacy. We need to be ready to take action and quickly transact the gospel.

I am surprised at how superficial and unreflective people tend to be. I am especially disappointed when that person is a professing Christian, because a Christian, more than anyone else, should excel at what I am talking about. This is the area of our expertise. We, of all people, should be good at identifying our sin, our sin, not the speck in someone else's eye, but the log in our own. Remember, your enemy is sin, not your spouse. When she sins, she is not the enemy, sin is the enemy. You must learn to recognize sin even while sin hides from you and tries to deceive you. You must put your gospel binoculars on, get out your Ten Commandments telescope, and be alert to identify sin. Even though sin hides, now and then you will see it raise its gnarly little head, and when it does you must grab it and name it: "This is sin."

Then when you identify your sin, take responsibility for sin. By naming it as sin, you are confessing it to be what it is: sin. You confess, that is, you say the same thing about sin that God says about sin. When you bring sin out of hiding and expose it under the light of the Word, you weaken its power. You contain and corner it. Now, exposed by the light of the law and the gospel, you can see sin in its true ugly destructive hideousness. Seeing the sinfulness of sin, you then resolve by grace, to turn from it, to repent of it. As Solomon wisely counsels in Proverbs 28.13, *He who conceals his transgressions will not prosper but he who confesses and forsakes them will find compassion*.

Christians should be skillful at this. This is what we do well. People know us as "believers," but it would be just as proper, and maybe even more potent, were people to call us "repenters." Identifying, owning, admitting, confessing and repenting of sin: that ought to be our specialty. Repentance is essential in our communion with God and repentance should characterize our dealings with each other, especially our most intimate relationships. Confession and repentance is what our God gives us in the gospel, and what He teaches us in our conversion, and what He calls us to as we continue to walk by faith with Him. He teaches us to live with each other in the same way that we are to live with Him.

Repentance expressed

Sadly, many fall short of true biblical repentance. When we experience a sense of conviction for wrongdoing, we often superficially satisfy our conscience by merely emoting. More often than not, when we sin we merely speak of our feelings. When someone does something wrong, what does he usually say? "I'm sorry." What is that? It is a statement concerning the person's feelings, their emotions. As a parent, I have tried to teach my children not to settle for mere sentimental repentance. It is fitting that we feel the pain of having sinned against someone and the words "I'm sorry" can express true remorse. But often we say those words flippantly, without any recognition of the travesty of our sin. Sometimes to show the inadequacy of such a response and to press my children to actually confess sin, when my son says, "I'm sorry," I respond by saying, "I'm hungry." My son has told me how he is feeling, so I tell him how I am feeling. I want to remind him that saying "I'm sorry" is not, in itself, a confession of sin. It is, perhaps, a statement of regret, which is legitimate and needful, but "I'm sorry" by itself is not true repentance. We need to move beyond the expression of mere feelings. If we are going to transact the gospel, we need to do more than merely exchange statements about our feelings.

Repentance involves confession. Instead of saying, "I'm sorry," we need to learn to say "I have sinned." We need to define sin as God defines it. That is what "confession" means: to say the same thing about sin that God says about sin. When I say biting cutting words, I need to recognize sin in my heart and the sin of my damaging words (cf. Matthew 15:18-20). My psychologized rationalizations do not change God's definition of my cruel speech. When I say things that are designed to hurt, I am violating the sixth commandment and using my words as a weapon. I need to confess, like my preacher-friend, "I've murdered that woman in my heart so many times." Murder? Are biting hurtful words really the moral equivalent of murder? Is that not an extreme interpretation of mere words? *You have heard that the ancients were told, 'You shall not commit murder.' And 'Whoever commits murder shall be liable to the court.' But I say to you that every one who is angry with his brother shall be guilty before the court; and whoever shall say to his brother, 'Raca,' shall be guilty before the supreme court; and whoever shall say, 'You fool,' shall be guilty enough to go into the fiery hell* (Matthew 5.21-22). When you use that word to inflict emotional pain on your spouse, you violate the sixth commandment.

Husbands, commands Paul, *love your wives, and do not be embittered against them* (Colossians3.19). The word *embittered* means to be sharp, caustic, or harsh. In other words, do not mistreat her or harm her. The opposite of embitterment in Colossians 3.19 is *love*. *So husbands ought also to love their own wives as their own bodies. He who loves his own wife loves himself; for no one ever hated his own flesh, but nourishes and cherishes it, just as Christ also does the church* (Ephesians 5.28,29). The opposite of love in Ephesians 5.28,29 is *hate*. To be embittered is a form of hatred, and hatred is the essence of murder. It is what Adam did, pointing his finger at Isshah: "Do you want to execute the death sentence on someone? Execute her." Harsh biting words are morally murderous.

Confess sin as sin. Do not excuse it or rationalize it. Grab the sin and subject it to the "qualitative analysis" of the law and the teachings of Christ. What moral quality of these words? Embittered, angry, hurtful words are, qualitatively, murder. When grace enables you to see *the exceeding sinfulness of sin* (Romans 7.13, KJV), grace also brings you to confess sin as sin. Bitterness is hate; hate is murder; murder is sin; therefore, confess bitterness for what it is. Say what God says about bitterness: it is sin. To confess is to agree with God and to speak of sin as God speaks of sin. You say what God says about your sin. You use God's measurement, his law, and you define sin as a violation of His law. When my words flayed her while I vented my anger, I was murdering her in my heart. I was sinning by breaking the sixth commandment. That is what God says, and that is what I must recognize.

Now that you have identified sin as sin and acknowledged it to be sin, you repent. You resolve, by grace, to put away wrath, anger, and clamor and to put on kindness and a disposition of love. Repentance is a one-hundred-eighty degree about face. It is a putting off and a putting on. It involves removing a vice and replacing it with its opposite virtue.

Repentance plants the opposite virtue in the precise place where the vice once grew. Repentance: this is the gospel commodity that the sinning party brings to the table to transact the gospel and to reenact his conversion.

Forgiveness bestowed

The sinning party brings the gospel commodity of confession with repentance. He admits his sin as defined by the Law of God, not merely expressing his emotional state of discomfort, not cheaply saying, "I'm sorry." Rather, the sinner brings genuine confession and repentance and asks for an exchange of gospel goods. He asks for forgiveness. He uses words to confess his sin, and he uses words to request what he wants in exchange for his confession: he wants forgiveness. So he asks for an exchange: "I give you my confession and repentance. Will you forgive me?"

Now the transaction requires the "innocent" party to contribute to the transaction. The one sinned against must now grant forgiveness. The sinner has offered repentance, now the offended party is to give the gospel commodity of forgiveness in exchange for the sinner's repentance. The offended one is to forgive, even as the Lord forgave him.

Again, we must delve beneath superficial sentiment. To forgive is to respond to the repenting sinner as our heavenly Father responds to us when we come to Him confessing our sin. How does He respond? He forgives us. That does not mean that He merely feels for us, but He takes action based on the work that Jesus Christ has done on the cross. He makes a legal application of the virtue of Jesus' shed blood and affirms His covenant love for us in which He makes us promises. The sacrifice of Jesus has propitiated[7] God's righteous wrath. God punished our sin once-for-all in the death of Christ.

The Father now glorifies His Son by treating us as He treats Christ Himself, when we simply exercise faith in Christ. For the sake of Christ and for the glory of His grace in Christ, He turns from wrath and grants grace, pardon, and forgiveness. In covenant love, He promises not to treat us as according to our sin, but to treat us in union with Christ, as justified, as righteous in Christ. For the sake of Christ Jesus, the Father accepts and forgives us.

Now we are to take that same gospel love, the love which the Father has for us in Christ, and in obedience to the Father, give His love to our sinning spouse. When I forgive my wife, I am not showing her my love as much as I'm showing her God's love. I am not giving her a love that I learned from my parents, or my school, or a love that naturally emerges out of my gene pool or aligns with my natural temperament. No. I give her the love which my Father has given to me in Christ. I give her God's love. Where do I get God's love? I obtain God's love at the cross of Christ. To forgive my wife I must go to the cross where Christ conquered the sin that now threatens my marriage. In the obedience of faith, I then take the love of God displayed on the cross and carry that gospel forgiveness by obedient faith to my sinning mate. In obedience to Christ, as a forgiven sinner myself, I give His love to my wife and together, as two disciples of Christ, we conquer our sin through the power of gospel love. Sin, you see, is ultimately against God and it is God who must ultimately defeat sin. With gospel love, we become weapons in God's hands through which He defeats the sin that threatens our intimacy. As we simply believe God and obey His gospel, His power works in and through us to overcome the sin that threatens intimacy and to enable us to experience a love that pulses with the life of the resurrection.

Jesus says that if we are His disciples, forgiveness is something we must do. We read in Luke 17.3- 4, *Be on your guard* - watch out, be careful, this is a point where we are vulnerable to attack - *if your brother sins, rebuke him and if he repents, forgive him and if he sins against you seven times a day and returns to you seven times saying, 'I repent,' forgive him*. Jesus says be alert when you live in close and continued contact with someone who is able to sin against you seven times in a day. Jesus is describing an intimate relationship, a relationship not unlike marriage. Proximity and intimacy inevitably occasion repeated sins which call for repeated gospel transactions.

If he says, 'I repent.' If he comes to the negotiating table and says, "I call you to negotiate gospel business with me. I want us to exchange gospel commodities. I come and confess my sin. I repent. I know I have sinned against you. Now I want you to engage me in a gospel transaction, a gospel exchange. I want you to forgive me. Will you forgive me?" Jesus says, "If he brings you to the table of gospel business, you must do business with him. Even if he asks for a gospel transaction seven times in a day, you must transact with him. When he offers repentance, you must receive his repentance and you must give him forgiveness in return."

No vengeance

When your spouse repents, you must transact the gospel and give her what God has given to you. You must give a believing application of the blood of Christ to the offense of the sin. You must enact the gospel, confident that Christ's blood has satisfied divine wrath and thus has removed any warrant for your personal vengeance. You must respond to the sinner's repentance and faith in Christ as your Father responds to the sinner who trusts in Christ. You must be reconciled through the blood of Jesus and, in gospel grace, make and keep gospel promises. To forgive is to promise to define your spouse as one united to Christ, not united to their sin. To forgive is to promise to rely on the power of the Holy Spirit, and to believe that the Spirit is at work to make the gospel effectual to transform both you and your marriage. In so doing, you imitate God as beloved children.

How does God respond when we confess our sin to Him? *If we confess our sins, He is faithful and righteous to forgive us our sins and to cleanse us from all unrighteousness* (1 John 1.9). We imitate God by responding to confession the way He does. *He is faithful*, not fickle, not arbitrary, not capricious, not unwilling, nor uncertain. My spouse should expect that when she seeks my forgiveness, I will give it. As gospel lovers, we are going to imitate our Father and be faithful and give gospel love.

He is faithful and righteous, which is to say that God acts legally. God responds to us when we confess our sin in keeping with the legal determination He made for us when He saved us and declared us to be righteous in Christ. He legally defines us in union with Christ and sees us as legally righteous because Christ made atonement for our sin by His death. He does not respond in wrath because He already satisfied His wrath against us in Christ. Now we are to imitate Him when our spouse sins against us. We are to treat our sinning spouse as our Father treats us; we are to view the sin as a sin for which Jesus died. We are to apply the grace of justification to our spouse and, on the basis of the finished work of Christ, forgive our spouse. We are to resolve our sense of offense in the realization that Jesus has borne the punishment for that sin, and it is not for us to contrive and execute a punishment of our own making.

Here is the challenge for the party who has been sinned against: relinquishing vengeance. When we are offended, we want to retaliate, to execute some form of punishment on the sinner. The response of anger to sin and the desire for punishment is not wrong, it is godly! Our temptation is to try somehow to resolve our anger and desire for punishment ourselves, instead of resolving our offence in God's provision of Christ's cross. We are tempted to usurp the place of God and to assume His prerogative to punish sinners. In so doing, we deny the sufficiency of Christ's cross. We forget that those harsh words which so hurt us, violated God's Law: His sixth commandment. The violation of God's Law is a concern far greater than our offended feelings. We are tempted to take the place of God and to make an idol of our offended feelings. We will not be at peace until our offended feelings are resolved. But the peace we should desire accomplishes more than merely making our bad feelings go away, it is a peace that resolves the problem of God's violated Law. We need the peace that comes from God; the peace that is based upon the work of Christ when He bore the punishment for our sins on the cross.

No matter how justified we may feel, if we vent our anger on our offending spouse, we blasphemously usurp the place of God and deny the efficacy of the cross. If we subject our offending spouse to "the silent treatment" and become emotionally or physically distant as a form of vengeful punishment, we act as though God's wrath was not propitiated by the cross. In effect, we tell God to step aside while we satisfy the demands of justice, not in the cross, but with our own form of punishment. But *the anger of man does not achieve the righteousness of God* (James 1.20). The execution of our contrived punishment is not an adequate basis for true and lasting reconciliation. Only in the cross of Christ is our sin fully punished. Only in the cross of Christ do we have the basis of true reconciliation. How many marriages turn cold and distant, even grind to an end, because the couple did not early on treat sin with gospel love but allowed a vengeful, unforgiving spirit to push the prospect of reconciliation away?

If the work of Jesus Christ on the cross is sufficient to appease the pure wrath of my holy and righteous God, then it must be sufficient to appease my inadequate sense of offense at my spouse's sin. I can satisfy my offended conscience knowing that God, whose law she broke, is propitiated by the blood of Christ. I, as His beloved and forgiven child, can likewise experience my anger being propitiated by the blood of Christ. The cross of Christ more than meets my demand to see sin punished. I can glory in the cross of Christ where the penalty for my and my spouse's sin was paid. I can relinquish a vengeful spirit, knowing that it is not my responsibility to contrive a punishment for my spouse. God has already punished Jesus on the cross for her sin. Therefore, if I respond in anger and give her "the silent treatment," or try to call down lightning from heaven on her, I am usurping the place of God. I am to be *righteous* in forgiving her, as my Father is *righteous* to forgive me (1 John 1.9). That is, I am to resolve the violation of sin in the righteousness of the cross and, based on the cross, I am to forgive her.

The challenge of the sinning party is to own the sin, but the challenge of the offended party is to let go of vengeance, to turn away from a retaliatory spirit. Just as owning and confessing sin is the challenge for the sinner, so the refraining from taking vengeance is the challenge for the offended one.

> *Never pay back evil for evil to any one, respect what is right in the sight of all men. If possible, so far as it depends on you, be at peace with all men. Never take your own revenge beloved, but leave room for the wrath of God, for it is written, 'Vengeance is Mine, I will repay,' says the Lord. 'But if your enemy is hungry, feed him, and if he is thirsty, give him a drink; for in so doing you will heap burning coals upon his head. Do not be overcome by evil but overcome evil with good*
>
> (Romans 12.17-20).

We must apply the legal blessings of our justification to each other in our marriage. We both stand on the righteous footing of Christ's atoning grace, His propitiating sacrifice. 1 John 4.10 defines love as the propitiating sacrifice of Jesus: *In this is love, not that we loved God, but that He loved us and sent His son to be the propitiation of our sin*. That is where we must stand together against our respective sin: on the propitiating virtue of Jesus Christ and His cross. Sin threatens to destroy the foundation of our love and separate me from my spouse. Sin would drive us apart by causing our consciences to demand that someone should punish the sinner. Our temptation is to assume that role, but that someone is God. If we assume the prerogative of God and judge and punish the sinner, then we only compound sin's destruction by disobeying the gospel's call to forgive each other even as God in Christ has forgiven us. We must believe God's gospel and the gospel says, "Christ satisfied God's just punishment for that sin. The moral foundation of your love is intact and secure in God's righteousness given to you in Christ. Now exchange the gospel commodities of repentance and forgiveness which God gave to you by faith in Christ, and come back together again in intimate love."

Think of your coat jacket's zipper as an illustration of the unity of your marriage. The higher the zipper, the more connected you are. The zipper moves up and down in the ebb and flow of spiritual, emotional, verbal, and sexual intimacy. But the bottom teeth, the foundational connection, are your consciences, your mutual trust of each other. Sin pulls the zipper all the way down and offends your conscience, destroys your trust, and rips the zipper all the way open separating the coat of your intimacy. In order to reconnect at those bottom teeth and move the zipper of intimacy back up, you must reconnect at the point of your consciences and your moral acceptance of each other. The gospel alone is sufficient to reconcile offended consciences and restore severed intimacy. When you transact the gospel and exchange repentance and forgiveness, you reconnect the bottom teeth of the coat of your intimacy. Now, with consciences at peace through the blood of Christ, you are at liberty to pull the zipper back up. You have granted honor to each other as fellow-heirs of the grace of life (1 Peter 3.7). Now not only are your prayers (intimacy with God) unhindered, but your intimacy with each other is also unhindered by the sin that you have conquered through gospel love. You stand anew on the foundation of gospel grace. Your intimacy is restored. Now you have the liberty and freedom to bring that zipper all the way up as far as it can go. As you learn to reconnect the bottom zipper teeth through gospel love, you will deepen your intimacy because you will delve into heart issues and come to know each other in private and intimate ways. Truly our God is gracious to teach us how to love each other as He loves us in Christ Jesus!

I PROMISE

Not only do we love each other by applying the grace of justification but we also apply the doctrine of sanctification to our marriage. In justification, we have the legal basis for reconciliation. In sanctification we have the benefit of the blood of Christ which also cleanses us from sin's defilement. In reliance on the promised grace and power of the Holy Spirit, we can look at each other with hope. The Spirit of Christ is at work in me, in my spouse, and in our marriage. We are learning to love each other in Christ. In Christ, my sinning spouse is a saint, holy and beloved. She is my gospel lover who, like me, is learning to love with the love that we have both received from Christ. Because Christ's blood is efficacious, because the Holy Spirit is working to complete that good work which God has begun in us (Philippians 1.6), we have hope.

Since the Spirit is working in us, enabling us to learn how to love with gospel love, we can express our hope in promises. Because of the faithfulness of the Spirit, we can hope to be faithful to our promises. When we forgive, we make covenant promises, like our Father, based on the efficacy of the blood of Christ. John tells us that the Lord is faithful and just to forgive us of our sin. The Lord makes us a promise. The Lord encourages us to confess our sin because we have His promise that He will forgive and cleanse us from all unrighteousness. So too, when I forgive my wife, I make promises to treat her as a justified sinner in Christ whom the Holy Spirit is actively sanctifying.

I promise that I will not continue to define her according to her sin, but according to the grace of Christ and the workings of the Spirit in her. In other words, I will not ruminate and mull over the sin, but I will rather refuse to allow myself to replay the offense in my mind. As one pastor friend of mine puts it, recollections of a forgiven sin can be like those internet "pop-up" advertisements that intrude onto your computer screen. When the thought of her sin pops into my head, I promise to hit the mental "delete button" immediately, and not to allow the pop-up to stay on the screen of my mind. I promise not to remind my spouse of her sin. I promise not to tell others of her sin. A true application of the gospel has resolved the matter. It may be necessary to revisit the incident wisely, graciously, and gently, to learn lasting lessons from what transpired, but not in order to reactivate the offense or to open an old wound which would threaten possible separation. With a humility rooted in the grace of the gospel, we can learn from our past mistakes, but we revisit them only to become wiser, not to make the same mistake twice.

We then work to produce the fruit of repentance. Together, the repenter and the forgiver work to bring this fruit to fruition. Often when dealing with each other's sin, you open matters of the heart in deep and profound ways. As you apply the gospel to the sins of the heart, you learn about each other in even deeper ways, and you grow as you tenderly minister grace to excise sin from one another's characters and conduct. Together you deepen your intimacy as you delve into each other's hearts with the confidence that you both will immediately treat the discovery of sin with the cleansing grace of gospel love.

The result of a gospel transaction to overcome sin is that you begin to experience the power of the resurrection in your marriage. Where sin once reigned in death, grace now abounds and conquers death experienced as separation. You experience more and more deep and thorough intimacy as you learn to love with gospel love. Through many genuine heart-to-heart exchanges of gospel love, you can pull up "the zipper" and reach new heights of intimacy.

I am thankful for my gospel lover. The Lord has enabled my wife to forgive me of deep heart stains. I have seen her act in faith and obedience to her Lord and treat me with grace, not according to my sin. I have seen the grace of God at work in her and have experienced God's grace being effective in her love for me. I have grown to trust her and to be confident in the Lord concerning her (2 Thessalonians 3.3-4). Our experience at the table of gospel transaction has enabled us to keep zipping the zipper of our intimacy higher and higher as we labor together in the unity that is ours in Christ. The times when our sin has invaded our intimacy have been opportunities to delve all the deeper into our hearts and apply the gospel in more penetrating ways. As we learn to love with gospel love, we come to new levels of trust, respect and intimacy. We learn to recognize God's grace working in and through us. As we perceive grace, we gain confidence that the Lord is, in fact, teaching us to love each other. We gain confidence that He will preserve our love as we endeavor to obey His gospel together.

Gospel love changes us. It makes us more holy. It gets us ready for heaven. I want to be able to meet my wife in heaven and have her come to me and say, "Thank you for the marriage we had back then. Thank you for loving me in the first creation. God used your love to help get me here. I will eternally rejoice in the God who taught us how to love each other with gospel love." That is what Paul talks about in Ephesians 5.25-27.

> *Husbands, love your wives just as Christ also loved the church and gave Himself up for her; that He might sanctify her, having cleansed her by the washing of water with the Word, that He might present to Himself the church in all her glory, having no spot or wrinkle or any such thing; but that she should be holy and blameless.*

That is what love does. It makes you more holy. Does someone love you? How do you know? Their love is impelling you to holiness.

How can two sinners experience this heart intimacy without their sin exploding and maiming or even killing them? Gospel love. Only Jesus Christ can teach us this love. He teaches us and we learn by practicing the gospel together. We are to seek intimacy, compelled by His grace, growing in holiness, and transforming our marriages into showcases of the triumph of the gospel. *And so, as those who have been chosen of God, holy and beloved, put on a heart of compassion, kindness, humility, gentleness and patience; bearing with one another, and forgiving each other, whoever has a complaint against anyone; just as the Lord forgave you, so also should you. And beyond all these things, put on love, which is the perfect bond of unity* (Colossians 3.12-14). In your marriage, be intimate and love each other with gospel love to the glory of God.

Discussion Questions for Chapter Eight:
The Transaction of Gospel Love

1. What makes a marriage a "Christian marriage?"

2. When did you learn how to overcome sin?

3. What is a gospel transaction?

4. What should be "our expertise" as Christians?

5. Why is saying "I'm sorry" often an insufficient expression of repentance?

6. What sin does Paul warn against by the word embittered in Col 3:19?

7. What is repentance?

8. How does forgiving require us to exercise faith in Jesus Christ?

9. When we forgive, whose love is being demonstrated?

10. What is “the challenge for the party who has been sinned against?”

11. How can the offended spouse resolve a sense of anger?

12. Explain how the doctrine of justification relates to the illustration of the zipper.

13. What are some of the promises the forgiver makes to the one forgiven?

14. How is it that overcoming sin with the gospel develops more intimacy?

15. How do you know if someone really loves you?

PART THREE:

OVERCOMING CHALLENGES TO MARITAL INTIMACY

Introduction

Who does not realize that we live in a day of unprecedented confusion, neglect and attacks against marriage? Heterosexuals do not want to enter marriage. Homosexuals want to "wed" (if you can use that term). The number of unmarried co-habiting couples is statistically at an all-time high. Biblical morality is under an intensified assault by radical homosexual activists who have infiltrated our American media, schools, and judiciaries. The Anglican-Episcopal church is on the brink of an international schism since the New Hampshire diocese ordained Gene Robertson, a practicing homosexual priest, into their bishopric. Legislators are deliberating a proposal to amend the Constitution to define marriage as between one man and one woman. Meanwhile, social agendas contrary to common grace and biblical norms continue to erode the moral foundation of western culture. It is a challenging time to stand for marriage, much less for Christian marriage.

Deceitful spirits promoting demonic doctrines aggressively seek to pervert and distort the glory of God our Creator. In 1 Timothy 4.1-5 Paul tells us of the strategy of the demonic. It is a strategy that targets the glory of God as Creator. Demonic doctrines cauterize men's consciences by convincing them to embrace perverse perspectives of the creation, specifically regarding marriage and diet. *Everything created is good*, writes Paul, but demonic deceptions work to obscure the essential moral goodness of the created order. People, believing demonic lies and distortions, then give themselves up to destructive lifestyles. He who is the liar and murderer (John 8.44) works especially hard to deceive people in these matters of the creation. We are seeing the effect of such deception in the widespread abuse of marriage.

Marriage has been under attack in our culture for several generations now. God is visiting the sins of our fathers on the third and fourth generation (Exodus 20.5). The clouds of demonic deception have long obscured our four guiding stars. Few are those who know the true and living God, and who therefore approach life as defined by the doctrines of God, Creation, the Fall, and Redemption. In a culture in which saltless Christianity prevails[8] and common grace[9] is decreasing, we are summoned to obey Christ and develop godly marriages which are characterized by gospel love and true intimacy.

In this final part of our study, we will consider some specific challenges to marital intimacy and ways that we can overcome them. This list of challenges comes from my personal struggles as well as observations from my pastoral experience. As daunting as these challenges may be, we can overcome them with gospel love. Learn to love with gospel love and you will *prove yourselves to be blameless and innocent, children of God above reproach in the midst of a crooked and perverse generation, among whom you appear as lights in the world* (Philippians 2.15).

9

The Challenge of Headship and Submission

LEADERSHIP: NOT 'SOURCE'

Ours is a day when words must struggle to retain any objective meaning. The serpent is still asking, *Indeed, has God said?* There are sinister strategies afoot designed to empty the words of the Bible of their biblical meaning. We must be on guard against those who would confuse us about the meaning of marriage and the terms used to define marriage.

Consider first, the biblical word and idea of "head" or "headship." Sadly, the modern virus of feminism has infected contemporary biblical scholarship. The feminist movement does rectify certain injustices for many women who are genuinely mistreated. Indeed, the most abused people on the planet are women, and Christians should be eager to deliver women from genuine injustice. However, feminism is often not so much about injustice as it is about empowering feminists. The power that feminists often seek is the power to "name the animals," a stewardship given to Adam in Genesis 2. Essentially, feminism is a rebellious commandeering of the right to define the meaning of words.[10]

One word that has come into disrepair is the biblical term

"head." Some modern lexicons[11] tell us that "head" can mean "source," as in the "head of a river." In other words, "head" means the originating point from which something begins. Theologians infected with the feminist virus bring this definition to texts like Ephesians 5.23: *For the husband is the head of the wife, as Christ also is the head of the church, He Himself being the Savior of the body.* They tell us that we are to recall how it was that God fashioned the woman from the rib of the man; that she originated from the man and so man is her source, her "head." Of course many of those who propose this perspective also view the early chapters of Genesis as myth, so the muddled meaning of "head" quickly gets murky. If all we are speaking about is a myth, then what does it mean or matter anyway? This feminized definition of "head" attracts those who willingly slight Scripture while trying to commandeer its authority to gain acceptance for their already-constructed convictions.

We will allow the Bible to define biblical terms. The Bible presents the feminist with a problem. Neither the Old Testament nor the New Testament ever uses "head" in a way that means "source."[12] Consistently, throughout the Greek Old Testament, the Septuagint, and the New Testament, the word "head" always has to do with "rule," "authority," and "exercise of government." Do not let anyone tell you otherwise. Wayne Grudem examined over 2,000 citations of the word "head" both in biblical and in classic Greek literature, and it never had the sense of "source." Still, the enticement to redefine this biblical word persists.

We must not redefine God's words to mean something more palatable to modern tastes. As married men, the Bible defines us as the "heads" of our homes. That is the role we have and that is our practical stewardship. The question is not, as the feminists frame it, "Is there such a thing as headship?" The husband is the "head." The question is, "Is the husband a good head or a bad head?" God designed marriage with a seat of authority and rule, a "head." God has assigned to men the stewardship of domestic government. The words "husband" and "father" are terms with inherent authority. To be a husband and a father is to have authority. The question is whether a married man or father is exercising that authority biblically, in a manner that glorifies God and benefits his wife and children.

SUBMISSION: NOT EGALITARIANISM

Second, we must allow the Bible to define the companion term to headship: "submission." Many today are also trying to transform the meaning of this word into something unbiblical. We see this in modern expositions of Ephesians 5.21. *And be subject to one another in the fear of Christ, wives to your husbands…* and so forth. Many today would have us think that Paul is calling for the mutual submission of wives to husbands and husbands to wives. Is this so?[13]

If we would understand what Paul means by being *subject to one another,* we must recognize how he arranges his argument in Ephesians 5.22 to 6.9. Verse 21 is a main heading in Paul's outline of thought, and introduces the section which follows. Here, in verse 21, Paul presents the action – *submitting to one another* – that he keeps in view throughout the ensuing verses. Beneath this main heading, he then shows how Christians are to obey this injunction to be submissive in three settings. In each of these settings, God has constituted human authority to which Christians are to submit.

The first setting is marriage in which the wife is to submit to her husband (5.22-33). The second setting is the family in which the child is to submit to the parent (6.1-4). The third setting is the workplace in which the slave is to submit to the master (6.5-9). In all three settings, Paul begins with the party that is to submit and then addresses the party that exercises authority.

We should also set the command to *be subject* of verse 21 in its preceding context. In verse 18, Paul commanded us to *be filled with the Spirit*. He then explains what he means through a series of five participles (those English verbs ending in "-ing" in verses 19-21). We demonstrate that we are filled with the Spirit by *speaking*, *singing*, *making melody*, *giving thanks* and *being subject* (literally "submitting"). The first four participles concern Spirit-filled worship. The last participle, *being subject* (submitting), concerns Spirit-filled living. Then in the following verses (5.22 - 6.9), Paul elaborates on the relationships in which Spirit-filled submission is to be worked out. We are to be filled with the Spirit by submitting to the God-appointed human authorities in our marriages, our families, and our vocational duties. Having learned what the Spirit-filled life should look like in the church (5.18-21), we then see what such a life should look like in the home (verses 5.22 - 6.9).

The verb *being subject* in verse 21 therefore serves as a hinge which swings the call to *be filled with the Spirit* (5.18) into the domestic realm. Interestingly, verse 22 has no verb of its own. The NASB has *be subject* in italics, which tells us that these words are not in the original Greek but were supplied by the translators to assist our understanding. In the original, the flow of Paul's thought is direct and unbroken:

being subject to one another in the fear of Christ - wives, to your own husbands as to the Lord. Paul is transferring the verbal idea of submission from verse 21 to verse 22 which he then opens up in the ensuing verses as we have seen.

We need to discern how Paul's thoughts interconnect here. The section on submission (5.21 ff.) immediately connects with the preceding section on being filled with the Spirit (5.18 f.). Paul explains what being filled with the Spirit looks like in normal life and human relationships. We who are being filled with the Spirit are not going to be living lives of insubordination to those human authorities which the Lord has placed in each of our lives. The life of worship in 5.18-20 is the life of submission introduced in verse 21 and explained in the following verses. In other words, if we give God Spirit-filled worship, then we will live Spirit-filled lives of submission to God's authorized human authorities. The life of worship is a life of submission.

What does this word *submit* actually mean? Furthermore, when Paul says, *be subject to one another,* is he describing a mutual submission where everybody is equally subject to everybody else? As the modern disease of feminism has made us liable to misunderstand biblical headship, the modern disease of egalitarianism similarly makes us liable to misunderstand biblical submission. Egalitarianism is the belief in the equality of all people. Equality is a legitimate virtue with many applications. The egalitarian, however, will often oppose any hierarchy of authority in a determination to equalize all people. There is an undercurrent of rebellion that runs beneath many of the egalitarian's arguments.

The egalitarian seizes on the words *one another* in verse 21 to advance his view of equality. He understands *be subject to one another* as urging two equal parties who are responsible to give mutual submission to each other. The egalitarian says that Paul is calling on Christians to be humble and to sacrifice voluntarily to meet the needs of others. This sacrificial service should be reciprocal and mutually granted by all Christians to all other Christians. Everyone is to submit equally to everyone else. To the egalitarian, verse 21 is one more of those "one anothering" verses that inform us about how we ought to foster unity among ourselves as believers. We thus obey verse 21 as we give and receive submission equally in a reciprocal and mutual exchange. The egalitarian does not want us to think of a hierarchy of position or exercise of authority in verse 21. And since Paul transfers the idea of mutual submission from verse 21 to verse 22, the egalitarian asserts that the same egalitarian dynamic of mutual submission should characterize the Christian marriage. If we apply the egalitarian definition of submission in verse 21 to marriage in verse 22, then we will not have male dominated hierarchical marriages. Instead, we would have "Christian" marriages in which both the wife and the husband equally submit to each other, that is, they endeavor sacrificially to meet each other's needs. The egalitarian says that we who speak of traditional biblical headship and submission are guilty of reading something into the text, of imposing our idea of authoritarian hierarchies on to verse 22.[14]

For example, Wheaton College professor Gilbert Bilezikian writes: "This reciprocity of such relationship renders hierarchical distinctions irrelevant within Christian communities of the church and family."[15] In other words, the church and the family are not hierarchies of authority. There is no headship; no authority posited in a position or office.

Thus there is nobody under whom someone should submit themselves. Mike Mason[16] says the husband's love in verse 25 is a synonym for the wife's submission in verse 22. In his reading, both "love" and "submission" have the same meaning: mutual submission. When he loves her, he submits to her, and when she submits to him, she loves him.

If submission does indeed mean "sacrifice one's self to meet another's needs," then we can see how that definition of submission aligns with the meaning of love. But submission is not synonymous with love. This redefined egalitarian interpretation of submission destroys what Scripture says elsewhere about the inherent order of God's creation, an order that still characterizes the home and the church.

We find the word "submission" used over forty times in the New Testament where it consistently means "placing under authority." This is the meaning of the words *be subject to one another* in verse 21. Paul is giving us a general rule which we must obey if we are going to live a Spirit-filled life. The Christian is to cultivate submission, that is, a voluntary willingness to take his place in those God-constituted hierarchies of human authority. Paul is aligning our behavior to the morality of the fifth commandment. Having expressed the general rule of voluntarily submitting oneself under God-constituted human authority, Paul then shows how we are to apply this general rule in practical terms. Biblical submission is to adorn the Christian in marriage, in family life, and in the workplace. The synonym for "submission" in verse 21 is not the word "love" in verse 25 as Mike Mason suggests. Its synonym is the word "obey" in 6.1 and 6.5.

Although the two Greek terms translated "submit" and "obey" are synonyms, there is an interesting nuance found in the voices of the verbs which Paul uses. The verb "obey" directed to children and servants (Ephesians 6.1,5) is an imperative in the active voice. But the verb "submit" in 5.21, which is implied in 22, and used again in verse 24 has a different voice. In these verses, "submit" is an imperative verb in the middle voice which is reflexive, that is, it calls for an action that refers back upon the actor himself. A reflexive verb underscores the voluntary nature of the action and assumes a certain benefit derived by the actor. This voluntary element is not as pronounced in Paul's dealings with children and servants. Peter O'Brien comments: "At the heart of this submission is the notion of 'order.' God has established certain leadership and authority roles within the family, and submission is a humble recognition of that divine ordering. The apostle is not urging every woman to submit to every man, but wives to their husbands. The use of the middle voice of this verb (cf. Colossians 3.18) emphasized that voluntary character of the submission. Paul's admonition to wives is an appeal to free and responsible persons which can only be heeded voluntarily, never by the elimination or breaking of the human will, much less by means of a servile submissiveness."[17]

Paul here expands and qualifies his teaching about our relationships to *one another*. We have to see who the "anothers" are with whom we are in relationship. Paul's idea of these relationships is not a simplistic, flattened, egalitarian one-size-fits-all duty. The submission in view depends on where God has providentially placed us in his created order of hierarchies of authority. The call to be subject one to another does not destroy the hierarchies of the home, the workplace, or the church for that matter. Here is the principle: *be subject one to another.* Paul then gives three specific examples of how we are to apply that principle in marriage, parenting, and the workplace. The injunction to *be subject one to another* does not remove the duties involved in being a wife, a husband, a child, a father, a servant, or a master. We are not to tear down the hierarchies which God judged to be good in creation to replace biblical authority with some feminized, egalitarian, vague and sentimentalized notion of "love."

As we live in submission to the various human authorities established by God, we are to realize that it is ultimately God Himself to whom we are submitting. Wives submit to husbands *as to the Lord* (5.22). Children obey their parents *in the Lord* (6.1). Fathers bring up their children in the discipline and instruction *of the Lord* (6.4). Slaves are obedient to their masters in sincerity of heart *as to Christ* (6.5). As we submit to human authorities, we do so as an expression of obedience to the Lord. The principle of submitting *as to the Lord* is expressed by Paul in 6.7 concerning the obedience of slaves: *with good will render service, as to the Lord, and not to men, knowing that whatever good thing each one does, this he will receive back from the Lord, whether slave or free.* This principle of submission applies to every legitimate expression of God-constituted human authority. When Paul addresses the subject of submission in Colossians 3.18-4.1, he states: *Whatever you do, do your work heartily, as for the Lord, rather than for men... it is the Lord Christ whom you serve.*

We need to examine ourselves here. Are you uncomfortable with all this talk of hierarchies and authority and submission? If so, that is because the world is influencing you more than Scripture at this point. We must *not be conformed to this world, but be transformed by the renewing of* our *mind*s (Romans 12.2).

Perhaps one reason a more egalitarian interpretation of *be subject one to another* might attract us is because today we see so few who exercise biblical leadership. Biblical leadership requires wisdom. The wise always exercise authority for the good of those who are led. Wise and loving leadership never degrades the person who has the subordinate role, but respects and honors those being led. James 3.17 describes wisdom's way as *reasonable,* willing to yield, willing to adapt without moral compromise. Christian husbands, fathers, bosses, and pastors need to lead wisely. While exercising headship, the husband is not like the Gentiles who "lord it over" men, but like Christ who got on His knees and washed men's feet. Interestingly, washing feet looks like submission; it looks like the behavior of a slave. Yet when Jesus finished washing their feet, what did He say? *You call Me Teacher and Lord; and you are right: for so I am* (John 13.13). Leading as a servant did not mean that Jesus was not in a position of rule or that He was not exercising authority. Rather, with the authority of Lord and Teacher, Jesus commands us to imitate Him, and wash one another's feet. To be like Christ, husbands must practice servant-leadership.

In Ephesians 5.21 to 6.9, Paul says in effect, "Submit to one another according to God-constituted human authorities. What I mean by that is, wife, submit to your husband; child, submit to your parents; and slave, submit to your master." He is not saying, "In the New Covenant we no longer concern ourselves with human authorities, which is to say, we no longer have husbands, or parents, or masters." How could he be saying that when he immediately addresses husbands, parents, and masters: those entrusted with authority? He does not dismantle authority structures. Rather, he injects the quality of the Spirit-filled life into these God-constituted hierarchies of human authority.

So, submit. Even after this exposition, are you still prone to bristle at the sound of the word "submit?" Submit, what a soothing word. Does not the mere sound of it make you feel warm and comfortable? No, it does not! It feels like somebody is trying to wrap barbed wire around me. Submit. Right away, I rear up. My teeth clench. My natural, fallen inclination is to rebel against authority – any and every authority. In sin I do not ask whether the authority is legitimate or whether it is being exercised lovingly, I immediately suspect it and set myself against it. But Paul, with apostolic authority, commands us to submit and directs us to learn submission from Jesus Christ.

CHRIST: THE MODEL OF HEADSHIP AND SUBMISSION

Paul arranges his words in 1 Corinthians 11.3 in an instructive way. He is addressing the issue of head-coverings in the church at Corinth. In verse 3 he says, *I want you to understand that Christ is the head of every man, and the man is the head of a woman, and God is the head of Christ*.

Paul teaches us that the gender distinctions which God established at creation are still relevant in the Kingdom of God. The community of the redeemed, the people of God who are alive even now with the life of the age to come, are to image God as male and female (Genesis 1.27) in this present age. In the church it is still necessary that women be women and men be men. Paul speaks about gender distinctions which come to their epitomized expression in marriage. Here again our four guiding stars direct us. Our marriages are to make a theological statement as we order them according to God's original design but imbue them with redemptive grace and love. Gender distinctions glorified God in creation and, now, infused with gospel love and redemptive purpose, those same distinctions glorify that same God, who is our Redeemer and Lord.

Notice how Paul has curiously arranged his presentation of headship. We have already used the term "hierarchy," another barbed wire word in our day. If I were to ask you to draw a diagram of the hierarchy of biblical headship and authority, how would you arrange it? Would you not start off with God at the top? Would your diagram place God who is head over Christ; then Christ who is head over the man; then the man who is head over the woman. Would you not probably arrange the diagram vertically, from top to bottom, like a "flowchart?"

Interestingly, when Paul is describing that hierarchy in verse 3 he does not present us with a vertical flowchart from the top down. Although he is referring to a hierarchy which he could rightly arrange from the top down, Paul starts in the middle of the diagram. He starts with Christ and the headship of Christ. We first learn that a Christian man is in submission to his head: Christ. It is this submissive disciple of Christ who Paul then presents as the head over the woman, his wife. His headship over her is an expression of his submission to Christ (compare Ephesians 5.23 ff.). As the woman's submission comes into view, Paul then points to the headship of the Father and the Son's submission. Thus Christ's submission becomes the defining point of reference for the woman's submission. She is to submit to the man's (that is her husband's) headship as Christ submits to His Father, and her husband is to exercise headship over her as Christ exercises headship over him. Paul arranges this hierarchy to set Christ forth as the model for both male discipleship and female discipleship, for we still follow Christ as males and females. As Christians, we image and glorify God in our created genders.

Paul connects us to this hierarchical arrangement of God-constituted authority in the middle, not at the top or at the bottom. In so doing, he keeps a constant focus on what it means for us as men and women to follow Christ. Christ is the pattern for the husband's headship. The husband's headship, therefore, is an exercise of submission, because the man exercises his headship knowing that Christ is his head. My headship is not whatever I want it to be. My headship must be like Christ's headship. The cross must condition the exercise of my headship. Gospel love must characterize the exercise of my headship. If I do not imitate Christ's headship over me in the exercise of my headship, I will inevitably exercise a "Gentile" headship, "lording it over" the one over whom I have authority (cf. Matthew 20.24-28). Authority in the Kingdom is not to have any such quality to it: its quality is derived from the cross. Only as I submit to the headship of Christ can I learn to exercise headship like Christ.

Christ is also the pattern for the wife's submission. Christ teaches her how to submit to legitimate authority by the way in which He submits to His Father in accomplishing our salvation. As I look to Christ to learn how to exercise my headship, my wife looks at Christ to learn how to exercise submission. She can display the unique nobility and beauty of her godly femininity as she follows Christ who lives in submission to His Father. Biblical wifely submission is not an effacement of her femininity but the means by which her femininity can flourish. From her position as wife and mother she can contribute to the home and society as only a wife and mother can. She is not to fall into the extreme of so submitting that she becomes an invisible entity in the home. Biblical submission is not a form of social suicide that removes my wife's presence. Submission does not mean that she is to wear a virtual veil over her face and lose her personhood. Submission does not mean that she has nothing to contribute. Biblical submission does not to rob our children of her mothering leadership nor rob me of the companionship and friendship that I need from her as my sister in Christ. As she takes her place in the family with Christlike submission, she assumes a crucial role enabling us to have a godly marriage and family. She learns how to perform her unique duties as a wife and mother from Christ. She is a disciple of Christ and she is to bear the fruit of her discipleship in her stewardships as wife and mother.

Christ is the pattern for both biblical headship and submission. The husband is to learn how to exercise his headship in submission to Christ. The wife is to learn how to be submissive from Christ. Christ becomes the focus of my discipleship as a husband, and my wife's discipleship as a wife. We are both disciples of Christ, and our genders qualify how we respectively follow Christ and prove our discipleship.

Paul applies the truth of headship to the situation at Corinth. This passage (verses 2-16) is filled with difficult and debated details. Whatever Paul was correcting, it had to do with a woman's adornment of her physical head which testified of her relationship to her male head, most likely her husband. Paul employs three arguments for the woman to have her head appropriately adorned: an argument from culture, an argument from creation, and an argument from the universal church's practice.

There is debate about just where a woman is *praying or prophesying* (verses 4-5). There is debate about just what the head-covering was: an article of clothing, a style of hair, a combination of both? How much does Corinthian culture condition our interpretation of this passage? Evidently there were ways that a woman could appear in public which were culturally recognized as *disgraceful*. Having her head uncovered, as having her head shorn of hair, conveyed such cultural disgrace (verse 6). Paul endorses and fortifies these cultural norms by anchoring them in the bedrock of God's created order in which God made men and women to be distinct and assigned each gender a different role (verses 8-11). Paul informs us that the order of creation still pertains to the conduct of Christian men and women. The fact that God created the man first (cf. 1Timothy 2:13), and that He made the woman for the man, is significant for the Christian. The moral order of creation is what is given expression through the cultural norms which visibly distinguish the genders, specifically by use of the head-covering. The angels, who only know God as Creator, and with whom we are involved in worship,[18] know that God is imaged as male and female, so for their sakes, we are to be gender-specific as disciples of Christ. *In the Lord,* however, the created interdependency of the genders is the more pronounced (verses 11-12). Paul's argument from *nature* (verses 13-15) could be an appeal which brings together his argument from culture[19] and his argument from creation[20]. Paul makes his appeals not only from cultural norms and the order of creation, but also from the universal practice of the churches (verse 16). The Christian church is to maintain the original creation's distinction of the genders in a culturally recognizable manner. The head-covering, be it an article of clothing, a hairstyle involving length of hair, or a combination of both, was such a culturally recognized symbol of distinctive femininity. The Christian woman is to adorn herself, and especially her head, in a manner that is recognizably feminine, both by angels who see God's image in creation and by pagans who see God's redeemed church in culture. All *the churches of God* are to have this sensitivity to matters of gender and culture.

Our interests are served by a consideration of 1 Corinthians 11.7: *For a man ought not to have his head covered, since he is the image and glory of God, but the woman is the glory of the man*. Here Paul transitions from his argument from culture to his argument from creation. He says that the cultural norm which does not require a man to cover his head while praying or prophesying (see verse 4) has a creation truth at its foundation: the man *is the image and glory of God*. Paul is not denying that a woman is also the image and glory of God, for that would contradict Genesis 1.27. His interests are focused on the significance of the head-covering which is appropriate for the woman but not for the man. The "key" to verse 7 is the word *glory*. Rather than being a disgrace to their respective heads (the covered man of verse 4 and the uncovered woman of verse 5 and 6), they are each to bring glory to their respective heads. To be the *glory of* someone means to bring honor, praise, and respect to that person. To "bring glory to one's head" is a phrase that means that our lives display the benefits of living under the rule and authority of that head. The citizens are the glory of their governors. The child is the glory of the parent.[21] The wife is the glory of her husband. The man, in his distinctive masculinity, is the image and glory of God the Creator. The fact that man was created first (verses 8-9) is at play in Paul's thinking. Before the woman was fashioned, the man displayed the glory of God as a man. How? He glorified God by the exercise of his headship, by assuming the responsibilities of the dominion mandate through his labor and his use of words. He lived under the headship of God by obediently, submissively, exercising his headship over creation. When the woman was formed, he exercised his headship over her as well. The way a man exercises his headship reflects back on his head: Christ. When a man leads like Christ leads, he is being submissive to Christ and Christ's rule over that man is seen to be glorious, honorable, and respectable. God is glorified when the man bears His image by exercising biblical, loving, servant leadership. Such Christ-like headship glorifies God because it is the result of the man's submission to Christ. Others see the benefits of his exercise of godly masculine leadership in his marriage and family. Thus Christ is honored as the head who leads the Christian man who then leads in a Christ-like manner. Thus by his godly headship, the Christian man lets his light shine before men in such a way that they may see his good works, and glorify his Father who is in heaven (Matthew 5.16).

In a similar way the woman *is the glory of the man*. As the man is the glory of God (that is, he manifests the benefits of being under Christ's headship), so too the wife displays the benefits of being under her husband's government. This is what Paul means when he says that she *is the glory of* her husband. When someone thrives and prospers under headship, they bring glory, honor, and respect to the one exercising that headship. The husband displays the benefit of being under Christ's government by governing his home with Christ-like leadership. By his obedient exercise of headship, in submission to Christ, he is *the glory of God*. The wife who blossoms and thrives under the headship of her husband likewise brings glory to her husband. Thus she, in her obedient exercise of submission, is the glory of man.

Do you want to see if a man is doing a good job as a husband? How can you tell if someone really is a godly and virtuous man? Look at his wife. If you want to see the quality of his leadership, you look at his "glory." You look at that which shows the effect of his leadership. You look at his wife. I am convinced that one of the most prominent qualifications for a man to be an elder or a deacon is his wife. If the man has any ability to impress someone else's soul for their spiritual good, we will see it in his wife because she is the most immediate evidence of his ability to lead. Can he impress his soul on others and stimulate their spiritual growth in grace? We will find the answer to that question in the woman with whom he is one flesh. His wife will show the quality of his rule. She will be his glory. The submissive husband whose submissive headship glorifies God can hope to lead a submissive wife, whose submission glorifies him. Headship issuing into glory – that is essential to God's purpose when He created headship.

The Christian woman is to embrace her privileges in Christ and in the church, not by disregarding her gender, but by elevating the purposes of God for her as a woman. She is not to think that being a new creation in Christ (2 Corinthians 5.17) means that she is no longer defined in terms of the original creation. She is not to think that because she is just as justified as a Christian man (see Galatians 3.28) and is *a fellow-heir of the grace of life* (1 Peter 3.7), that God's order for the genders are thereby rendered null and void. No. We still inhabit this created realm in which we marry and are given in marriage. It is not until the resurrected state that marriage will no longer pertain (Matthew 22.30). Meanwhile God's original ordering of the genders, an order which is still evident by common grace in human cultures, has abiding relevance. As the godly wife exercises her gifts and engages in her ministries among the people of God, she does so as a woman whose life of submission brings honor to her godly husband, whose submissive headship brings honor to Christ. Thus Christ is the model for both headship and submission.

Discussion Questions for Chapter Nine:
The Challenge of Headship and Submission

1. What doctrine is especially assaulted by Satan according to 1 Timothy 4.1-5?

2. What is the two-fold essence of feminism?

3. What commonly held definition of "head" should we reject?

4. How does the Bible define "head?"

5. What is the question that every husband must answer about headship?

6. What is a commonly held misinterpretation of Ephesians 5.21?

7. Identify the outline of Paul's argument in Ephesians 5.18-6.9.

8. How do egalitarians define "submit" and what is the implication of this definition?

9. Is "submit" a synonym for "love?"

10. What is the function of Ephesians 5.21 and which of the Ten Commandments is at issue?

11. If "love" is not a synonym for "submit", what is its synonym in Ephesians 6.1 and 6.5?

12. What is the nuanced difference between the obedience of a wife and that of a child?

13. Who are the "one anothers" in Ephesians 5 and 6?

14. What does biblical leadership look like?

15. What from creation is still relevant for Christians according to 1 Corinthians 11.3?

16. What is unusual about Paul's "flowchart" of headship in 1 Corinthians 11.3, and how does Paul's approach inform us of the husband's submission and the wife's submission?

17. What three arguments does Paul use in 1 Corinthians 11.1-16?

18. What does it mean to bring glory to one's "head" in 1 Corinthians 11.7?

19. How should the husband uniquely glorify God in a way that differs from the way the wife glorifies God?

20. What is Paul speaking of when he says that the wife is *the glory of the man*?

10

The Challenge of Selfishness

THE ATTITUDE OF CHRIST

Selfishness is the second challenge to marital intimacy that we will consider. Think of a couple which has run into marital problems because they were both too selfless, too humble. Couples have marital difficulties, more often than not, because one or both of them, in some way shape or form, is being selfish. "Love yourself. Forgive yourself. Be good to yourself. Gain self-esteem. Indulge yourself. Enjoy yourself." Such are the attitudes of the world. But we are to have the attitude of Christ as Paul instructs us in Philippians 2.1-8.

> *If there is any encouragement in Christ, if there is any consolation of love, if there is any fellowship of the Spirit, if any affection and compassion, make my joy complete by being of the same mind, maintaining the same love, united in Spirit, intent on one purpose. Do nothing from selfishness or empty conceit, but with humility of mind, let each of you regard one another as more important than himself. Do not merely look out for your own personal interest, but also for the interest of others. Have this attitude in yourselves which was also in Christ Jesus, who although He existed in the form of God did not regard*

equality with God a thing to be grasped, but emptied Himself, taking the form of a bondservant, and being made in the likeness of men. And being found in appearance as a man, He humbled Himself by becoming obedient to the point of death, even death on a cross.

We are to have the attitude of Christ in our church fellowship, but we should cultivate and practice this attitude in our homes and especially in our marriages. As we practice Christ's attitude in our marriages, we can instruct our children in the attitude of Christ and then transfer that set of relational skills into our dealings with others in our church and society.

In Philippians 2.1-2 we see a description of the unique unity that is ours in Christian love. Paul uses a marvelous word in verse 2 which we translate with the three English words *united in spirit*. The Greek word means to be in full agreement, harmoniously united. The word describes a deep unity of soul; to be one in spirit. The Greek word places the prefix "sym" on the root word for "souls." Our English word "symphony" is similar: the harmonious blending of sound. Here Paul describes the harmonious blending of souls. A marriage characterized by self-denying gospel love will produce a knitting of souls: souls in symphony.

In verses 3 and 4, Paul calls us to put off *selfishness*. This word speaks of manipulating others for one's personal advantage. To the first century Greek, the term "denoted a self-seeking pursuit of political office by unfair means. It then came to be used of party squabbles, of the jockeying for position and the scheming for place and power. Finally, it meant the ambition which has no conception of service and whose only aims are profit and power."[22] We are also to put away *empty conceit*. This is an inflated, false view of one's self. This word "refers to one who attempts to achieve unfounded respect by big talk, boasting, and ambition."[23] We read in Romans 12.3, *For through the grace given to me I say to every man among you not to think more highly of himself than he ought to think, but to think so as to have sound judgment, as God has allotted to each a measure of faith.*

Then Paul calls us to put on *humility of mind*. This is a compound word which joins "lowly" and "mind." So much depends on our attitude. Paul wants us to be *of the same mind* in verse 2, and to have the *mind* (attitude) *of Christ* in verse 5. Only as we see ourselves in relation to God can we cultivate this lowliness of mind. This is not a self-deprecating morbidity. Rather it is an accurate self assessment made before God. We are noble creatures who have been made in the image of God, who, although sinful, are yet granted grace and given the privilege to live for the transcendent purpose of the glory of God. *Humility of mind* is an attitude that appreciates the dignity of who we are in Christ and perceives that we, like Christ, are to live for the higher purpose of God's glory, not the immediate gratification of selfish impulses. The humble man embraces the greatness of the Kingdom, knowing that to be great in the Kingdom of God means being the servant of all (cf. Luke 22.24-26). *And so, as those who have been chosen of God, holy and beloved, put on a heart of compassion, kindness, humility, gentleness and patience* (Colossians 3.12). *With all humility and gentleness, with patience, showing forbearance to one another in love* (Ephesians 4.2).

With this attitude of heart, we are then to *regard one another as more important than* (ourselves). "To regard" means to form a judgment based on a decision. We are to decide to judge one another, especially our spouse, in terms of God's grace. We are to judge one another in the light of the gospel. We see each other illuminated in the light of the character of our heavenly Father. We judge one another in the light of His love for us in Christ and His work in us by His Spirit. *From now on, we recognize no man according to the flesh* (2 Corinthians 5.16). We *regard* and define others according to the grace of God. Knowing that we are wonderfully loved and blessed in Christ, we are freed up from the burden of having to care for ourselves. God our Father cares for us. Instead of expending our interests on ourselves, worrying about what we shall eat or what we shall drink or wear (Matthew 6.25-34), we are liberated to be like Christ, and to serve others. We are called to be like Jesus, who *knew that the Father had given all things into His hands,* He then girded Himself as a servant to wash the feet of others (John 13.1-5). When we are confident that God is taking care of us, we are liberated to administer God's care and love to others. Paul tells us to *look out for… the interests of others*. The English word "scope" is taken from the Greek term which is translated *look out for.* We are to survey the landscape of our lives like a hunter looking through the scope on his rifle, taking aim at every opportunity to meet the needs of others. If we are to relate like this to our brethren in the church, how much more to our spouse with whom we are one flesh?

This *humility of mind* is revealed by Christ Jesus and we are to put on His *mind,* His *attitude* (Philippians 2.5). Philippians 2.5-8 presents us with some of the most challenging words in the New Testament, not only because they challenge us to humble Christlikeness, but because the passage itself contains difficult words and concepts to interpret. In the midst of the challenge to exegete these words, we cannot forget that Paul is pointing to Christ as the supreme example of humility. The second person of the Godhead humbled Himself by becoming a man and assuming responsibility for the salvation of His people. For the interests of others, He was obedient to His Father and accomplished the Messianic mandate by dying on the cross to atone for our sins. Here is humility! We must go to Christ if we are to learn humility of mind, for only He is *gentle and humble in heart* (Matthew 11.29).

Discipleship and self-sacrifice

Who is it that responds to Christ call to come to Him and learn humility from Him (Matthew 11.28,29)? Disciples. Who are disciples? They are those who, by faith in Christ, deny themselves, take up their cross daily, and follow Christ (Luke 9.23). The disciple's faith in Jesus outweighs his sinful love of self. He willingly takes up his cross, identifies with the crucified Lord, and puts his sinful selfishness to death. Paul describes this aspect of discipleship as being "crucified with Christ." *Our old self was crucified with Him, that our body of sin might be done away with, that we should no longer be slaves to sin* (Romans 6.6). *I have been crucified with Christ; and it is no longer I who live, but Christ lives in me; and the life which I now live in the flesh I live by faith in the Son of God, who loved me, and delivered Himself up for me* (Galatians 2.20). *Now those who belong to Christ Jesus have crucified the flesh with its passions and desires* (Galatians 5.24). Only through union with Christ can the believing disciple overcome the challenge of sinful selfishness.

As disciples of Jesus, we obey the summons to self-denial in our marriages. Jesus calls us to self-sacrificial service in marriage. He calls us to die to self-interest so that we might minister grace to our spouse. Marital intimacy demands this profound self-abandonment because, of all human relationships, only marriage delves so deeply into our souls and lasts for such a long time. The challenge to mortify selfishness is constant throughout the course of our entire lives. At different stages in life we face this challenge to mortify selfishness in fresh and unprecedented ways. Yet at every stage, it will be the same familiar challenge posed by our selfishness. The circumstances of life will change and we ourselves will change, but we will continually contend with two powerful centers of self-assertion: the husband and the wife. Two assertive selves will constantly collide as we try to negotiate and navigate an intimate knitting of one another's souls. We will only make progress as these two centers of self-centeredness eradicate their individual selfishness in order to draw near to one another in a common commitment to Christ.

A Christian marriage is the marriage of two disciples who are each resolved to deny themselves and follow Jesus. Self-denial and self-sacrifice will therefore, characterize their love for each other. If a marriage is to display gospel love, the two married disciples must both crucify the sin of selfishness and learn to give each other sacrificial love.

Sacrificial love is described for us in Ephesians 5.25-27.

> *Husbands, love your wives, just as Christ also loved the church and gave Himself up for her; that He might sanctify her, having cleansed her by the washing of water with the word, that He might present to Himself the*

church in all her glory, having no spot or wrinkle or any such thing; but that she should be holy and blameless.

Paul has just commanded the Christian wife to submit to the headship of her husband as the church submits to the headship of Christ (verses 22-24). Now, addressing the Christian man as the head in the marriage, Paul commands him to love his wife as Christ. Here is the essence of his leadership: love. The Christian husband leads by loving. That truth must sink in. Christian leadership is not tyrannizing, domineering, or manipulating. Christian leaders lead by loving. Paul speaks of a specific love; a love that takes initiative, that is, a love that leads. The love that Paul speaks of is a determined love. The lover has decided to love. He loves, not as a response to what is lovable, but as an expression of his resolve. He is determined to love because he is who he is. Gospel love is a love in which we are the actors, taking initiative to do what love does.

The Christian husband does for his wife what Jesus does for His church: *He gave Himself up for her.* He sacrificed Himself to fulfill all that was previously pictured by the Old Covenant sacrifices. The Christian husbands love is not atoning, like Christ's, but it is to imitate His act of self-sacrifice. The attitude of Christ described in Philippians 2.5 is expressed in acts of self-sacrifice. The husband is called upon to sacrifice many of his personal preferences *for her*, rather than to indulge in them for himself.

Self-sacrificial love has a purpose: *that He might sanctify her.* Gospel love seeks to make the one loved more holy. Self-sacrificial gospel love stimulates us to become more like Christ. Self-sacrificial love is willing to deny self-gratification in order to promote those things that will *cleanse* and foster godliness in the character and conduct of the one loved. Holiness is pursued by self-sacrificial acts and by *cleansing* words: *by the washing of water with the word*. Our words, the Greek here specifies verbal speech, is to have a cleansing, washing effect on the soul of the one we love. Earlier in Ephesians 4.15 Paul tells us that we will grow into Christlikeness as we *speak the truth in love*. Gospel love acts and talks. It speaks words of truth: what is biblically true and what is honest and real. The husband, who would love his wife as Christ loves the church, will endeavor to talk to her with words of Scriptural truth, communicating honestly, transparently, from the heart. This is how God communicates to us. He is the God who acts and speaks to reveal His love. We are to imitate Him as we strive to love each other.

Ironically, self-sacrificial love that seeks to sanctify does not result in frustration, but in satisfaction: *that He might present her to Himself*. Yes, Jesus *gave Himself up* for His church, but His bride, now sanctified by His love, is presented to Himself. The self-denying lover is ultimately satisfied by having a bride who is glorious, *without spot or wrinkle, holy and blameless*. We too are called to sacrifice ourselves in hope! We love sacrificially, hoping that our love will benefit our spouse. We love sacrificially, anticipating and experiencing the profound satisfaction of a love that gratifies and is glorious. We invest in that love by self-sacrificial acts and sanctifying words and our investment is well spent for we are given the profound satisfaction of loving and being loved with gospel love.

Wisdom from above

Marriage is a daily call to deny self. It is a particular path of discipleship. It is an arena in which we are to die to self and to live in the power of the resurrection. Our marriage is now the primary stage on which we live out our discipleship to Jesus Christ. It is in our marriages that we follow Christ. It is in our marriages that we learn to mortify selfishness. It is in our marriages that we enjoy and experience the resurrection power of the gospel and the triumph of gospel love. In marriage we learn to cultivate sacrificial love in the little things: yielding, relinquishing, and submitting to Christ. James tells us in James 3.16-17 *for where jealousy and selfish ambition is, there is disorder and every evil thing. But the wisdom from above is first pure then peaceable, gentle, reasonable* (which means "willing to yield"), *full of mercy, good fruits, unwavering, without hypocrisy*.

How can our marriages fulfill these biblical injunctions? We must navigate our marriages by the light of the guiding star of redemption. We must take the way of the cross and learn from Christ how to die to self. Then, being dead to self in Christ, we will rise to newness of life with Christ. In living union with Christ, we can then live as servants, ministering Christ's love to our spouse. We cannot love like this in and of ourselves. This kind of love is not our love. This love does not emerge from us. It is the love that we have received from Christ and it is His love that He calls us to give to each other. Sometimes I'm told, "Look, Pastor, I can't. I can't do this. I didn't learn how to do this as a child in my home. My parents gave me a bad example. I have unhappy memories." Stop defining yourself with the psychological blame-shifting of a generation trained in the babble of therapy culture. You are a new creation in Christ! Define yourself in Christ. The first command given in the epistle to the Romans is Romans 6.25. After over five chapters of instruction on our union with Christ, Paul finally tells us to do something. *Even so, consider yourselves to be dead to sin, but alive to God in Christ Jesus*. Believe in Christ and know who you are in Christ. You have the Holy Spirit and you have been given the spiritual equipment to love. God loves you in Christ Jesus! Now take His love and give it to your wife! Give His love to your husband! Imitate God and give God's love to each other. Follow Christ and experience His love being given and received as husband and wife. Learn His love and then live His love as you practice loving each other in the power of His Spirit. Live by faith in Christ and you will make progress in overcoming your innate self-centeredness as disciples of Christ. Deny yourself. Sacrifice yourself for your spouse. Seek to sanctify your spouse with your loving deeds and words. And receive the satisfying joy of gospel love.

Discussion Questions for Chapter Ten: The Challenge of Selfishness

1. What kinds of attitudes are involved in selfishness and empty conceit (Philippians 2.3)?

2. What kind of attitude is involved in humility of mind?

3. What do to regard and to look out for mean?

4. How does Christ exemplify humility of mind?

5. What aspects of discipleship and union with Christ are necessary to overcome selfishness?

6. The challenge posed by selfishness continues throughout our lives because "we will continually contend with ______________" [fill in the blank].

7. What kind of love is the Christian husband to give his wife according to Ephesians 5.25-27?

8. For what purpose does the Christian husband love his wife?

9. What will result when a Christian husband loves his wife?

10. In what ways will the "wisdom from above" benefit our marriages?

11. When a Christian says "I cannot love like this," how can we encourage him?

11

The Challenge of Unbiblical Communication Patterns

Meaningful words

Few skills are more important for a healthy marriage than the skill of wholesome, biblical communication. Central to the skill of communication is the use of words. Once again, if we would understand how to use words, the guiding star of creation must direct us. The Word of God is the explanation for creation and for man, His image-bearer, who is uniquely the "word-creature." In the male-female relationship, words play a crucial role. Words and their meaning lay at the crux of the Fall. In redemption, the Word is again God's agent of salvation. God gives us the Word who became flesh (John 1.14), and the Word of Scripture, and He yet speaks in the foolishness of the preaching preached (1 Corinthians 1.21).

The main action throughout the week of creation is that of the speaking God. As you read Genesis 1, you encounter God's speech as the means by which God brought creation into being (compare John 1.1-3). With His words, the speaking God created, formed and filled His universe. Repeatedly we read *God said, God said, God said, God called, God called*. Our Creator is The Speaker whose words are effective and give meaning.

In Genesis 2 we meet the Creator's image, the word creature: man. Before the woman's creation, this word creature received a stewardship for three kinds of words. First, God gave him "creation words." These were God's definitions by which Adam learned of the trees and their purpose (Genesis 1.29-30).

Second, God gave him 'Sabbath words.' *The Sabbath was made for the man, not the man for the Sabbath*, Jesus says in Mark 2.27. But where are these Sabbath words in Genesis? Moses says that *God blessed and sanctified* the Sabbath (Genesis 2.3). When you bless somebody, what do you do? You speak. We do not have the record of what God said, but in Genesis 1.28, we learn that for God to bless, God speaks: *God blessed them, and God said to them*. We can assume then that when God blessed the Sabbath, He uttered words. He blessed the Sabbath. He attached words to that day and then He *sanctified it*. To sanctify essentially means to set something apart to the Lord himself. How are we to understand sanctity during the time before sin and the Fall? How would God sanctify this day? He sanctified the Sabbath and associated it with His own Person and Presence. He sanctified the Sabbath day by His own presence. On the Sabbath, God gave Himself to Adam and entrusted him with Sabbath words.

Third, He gave Adam 'law words' when He commanded him not to eat of the forbidden fruit (Gen 2.17).

After this Adam, the word creature, the Definer, the steward of words, exercised his headship by naming all the animals. When Eve came on the scene, Adam immediately named her. He acted as God made him to act in his stewardship of words and defined the woman. Indeed, when the woman came on the scene, everything had already been named and defined.

Words give meaning to all creation. The stewardship of words and the responsibility to define accurately in obedience to God's words is a responsibility given to us men in particular. In practical terms, we give meaning to our wives and our children through our words. Our words fashion the world in which our family lives. If we call our children "idiots," they will likely believe our definition of them and start acting out the meaning of our words. We have the power of defining. They live in the world that we define for them.

Cleansing words

In Ephesians 5.26, Paul uses an interesting term when he speaks of Christ *having cleansed her with the washing of water with the word*. We derive our English word "rhetoric" from the Greek term which is here translated as *word*. Paul uses vocabulary that specifically refers to the spoken word. By this term, Paul gives us insight into how a man is to sanctify his wife. He is to sanctify her by speaking edifying words which wash her and communicate gospel grace to her.

We must recognize the unique value and importance of verbal communication. I can only touch on a couple of exhortations. Gentlemen, you have to talk. We need to speak to our wives and families. I am convinced that what attracts a woman to a man is his words. Gentlemen, our biceps, which soon become bye-bye-ceps, are not what opens her heart. Our money, which often takes wings and flies away, is not what opens her heart. What opens her heart? Words. Her heart opens to a man who has the ability to give meaning to her by speaking to her. By his words, a man assures her that he understands the world and that he understands her. His words give her security, define her role and map out the course of action for what lies ahead. What she needs is a man who understands life and can lovingly communicate with words. Your words, gentlemen, are the descending stairway into the depths of intimacy.

Men, you must monitor and regulate the words that are spoken in your house. You are the verbal thermometer. The head of the family must set the verbal temperature and take responsibility for the verbal climate of the home. The head is responsible for whether there is singing or arguing going on in the kitchen. I have my study in my home. As I age, my hearing is getting worse and I cannot always hear what is being said, but I can recognize the melody line of the conversation. I know whether the house is singing in a minor key or a major key. When I hear the minor key, I need to come out of my study and, like a conductor tapping his baton on the music stand, try to get all the instruments to play pleasantly in a major key. Sometimes, I confess, it is my voice that injects the note that forms the minor chord. Nevertheless, I am responsible for the verbal atmosphere of my family. We have to monitor the verbal temperature in our homes: whether there is politeness or peevishness, whether we are being encouraging or unduly critical.

Not only are we to supervise the verbal climate, but we are to insist that our families use specific vocabulary. Beyond the courtesies of "please," and "thank you," which are themselves disappearing from our daily discourse, we must insist on the use of gospel terms, gospel words. People today are more familiar with the terms of therapy than they are the terms of theology. As Christians, we should speak to each other theologically. Speak theologically by conducting family worship, by constantly leading your family in spontaneous prayer. Engage in gospel transactions all the time. Sin erupts persistently, so we must persist in doing gospel business with one another. We should continually be exchanging gospel commodities. There it is, that harsh word, that act of selfishness. You see it, so you step in to direct your family to resolve the potential division caused by sin. You direct your family in the use of specific gospel vocabulary. "I'm sorry," my child says. "No," I respond, "say, 'I sinned.' Tell me what sin you committed and ask me to give you my forgiveness." When sin erupts, let the gospel abound even more as your household continually learns gospel love and how to deal with sin as sin with the vocabulary of Scripture, not the feelings-oriented drivel of this self-consumed self-analyzing culture. Let us speak like Christians in our homes. You see, if we are not Christians in our homes, we are not Christians.

Affectionate words

Ephesians 5.28-29 says, *Husbands, love your wives. No one ever hated his own flesh but nourishes and cherishes it just as Christ also does the church because we are members of His body*. What is the opposite of *hate*? Yes, Paul uses the word *hate*: *no one ever hated his own flesh*. Maybe you where a little astonished earlier when you read of my friend who confessed that he has murdered his wife in his heart. "Murder" is a strong word. Well, that is what Paul is saying here. Do not hate your wife. Hatred is essentially murder. The opposite of hating is *nourishing and cherishing*. *Nourish* means to develop to maturity and fruitfulness. *Cherish* means to warm something up to the place that it softens. That is an interesting idea. In other words, cultivate warmth and affection in your communication with your wives. Not to do so, is to deprive your wife of the nutrients and care that she needs for her very life. Not to nourish and cherish your wife is starve her, which is a form of murder.

Willard Harley identifies five prominent needs among those whom he has counseled over the years. He says the first and primary need for husbands statistically, according to the polls taken, is for sex. The first need for the wife is for affection. "To most women, affection symbolizes security, protection, comfort and approval, vitally important commodities in her eyes."[24] He goes on to say (and men need to learn this), "Women find affection important in its own right. They love the feeling that accompanies both the bestowal and the reception of affection, but it has nothing to do with sex. Most of the affection they give and receive is not intended to be sexual. This confuses the typical male. He sees showing affection as part of sexual foreplay."[25]

Ladies, for your husband to be affectionate and for that affection not to lead into physical intimacy will usually feel like self-denial to him! It feels like cross-bearing. But that is the way in which he is to cherish his wife, to warm and soften her, because she needs to be cherished, and not simply as a maneuver into physical intimacy.

Perhaps you have seen a picture that has circulated on the Internet of two electronic machines depicting the difference between a man and a woman. A simple little bare, undecorated metal box with a single "on-off" switch represents the man. The woman is depicted by this big electronic control board with dials, controls, levers, and knobs. Many men have a simplistic flick-switch approach to sex: give affection - get sex. But Paul says *nourish and cherish* her to for the glory of Christ, not as a button to push on the vending machine of sex. *Nourish and cherish her.* Such Christ-honoring love will always involve the self-denial of discipleship. Harley suggests several ways to show affection: hugging, greeting cards, flowers, dinner out, opening the door for her, holding her hand, walking after dinner, back rubs, phone calls, conversations. In other words, show her some good old fashioned romance.

Sexual communication

Having acknowledged that a husband should not merely show affection as a prelude to sexual foreplay, we should note a connection between these two foremost female and male needs. Again, Harley says, "When your marriage is struggling sexually, look for the missing element of affection. Without the environment, the sexual event is contrived and unnatural for many women. All too often she reluctantly agrees to have sex with her husband even though she knows she won't enjoy it."[26] "Without (affection) a woman's sexual experience is incomplete."[27] "Affection is the environment of the marriage while sex is an event."[28] We have seen that the husband is responsible for the environment of affection. Harley goes on to assert, "Most affairs start because of a lack of affection for the wife and a lack of sex for the husband."[29] When couples deprive each other of these needs, they can descend into a vicious cycle. He shows no affection. She shows no interest in sex, which lessens his ability to be affectionate, which separates them further physically. They veer away from intimacy into separate emotional worlds and are vulnerable to resentment, insensitivity, hatred, to death.

This brings us to consider sexual communication in marriage. This area of intimacy is much more meaningful and immense than we usually think. We need direction from all four guiding stars to navigate these waters.

We need to direct our sexual intimacy by the light of the guiding star of theology. Our physical intimacy is an incarnation of the intimate fellowship of the Triune God.

We need to direct our sexual intimacy by the light of the guiding star of creation. God created sex as good. We see moral beauty in the picture of the man and his wife at the end of Genesis 2, who are both naked and not ashamed.

Yet we also need to see our sexual intimacy in the light of the Fall because the couple severed their sexual intimacy with those fig leaves, covering their genitals. Sexuality lies at the crux of the tragedy of the Fall.

Then, the guiding star of redemption reveals that a Christian couple's sexual intimacy has redemptive significance. The moral beauty of the original creation is still to be seen in the Christian's marriage. When Paul teaches us about Christian marriage in Ephesians 5 as a showcase of Christ's love for His church, he anchors our understanding of marriage in Genesis 2.24 which he quotes in verse 31. *For this cause a man shall leave his father and mother, and shall cleave to his wife, and the two shall become one flesh. This mystery is great*. Mysteriously, marvelously, we who learn to love each other with gospel love still display that original beauty, now incorporated and elevated by the gospel to glorify Christ.

We need to heed God's exhortation on marital intimacy which He gives us in Hebrews 13.4: *Let marriage be held in honor among all and let the marriage bed be undefiled for fornicators and adulterers God will judge*. All are to honor marriage as an institution. All are to esteem, respect and value marriage. We are to revere the essential emblem of marriage which is *the marriage bed*. The Greek term *marriage bed* transliterates into the English word "coitus" which means sexual intercourse. *The marriage bed* is a synonym, or rather a discreet euphemism, for sexual intercourse. God says all are to honor sexual intercourse and keep it *undefiled*. *Undefiled* is a term that has to do with Old Covenant ceremonial cleanliness and moral purity: that which is without stain or corruption. Sex in marriage is sanctified. It is without stain. It is holy and acceptable to the God who created it and gave it to man.

Have you ever thought of God being present with you in your bedroom while you are being physically intimate with your spouse? What is your response to that thought? If you are thinking biblically, that is an exhilarating and ennobling thought. In your one flesh intimacy, you are revealing something about God Himself. You are enjoying the intimacy that He has given to you as a reflection of His own Triune being. He delights in you as you delight in each other as He beholds His image reflected in your intimacy. He made you to be one flesh and He views your physical love as something good in His good creation. He delights to see a depiction of His own Son's love for His Bride mirrored in godly gospel-saturated marriages. Give sex its theological significance and it then becomes the hallowed, precious blessing that God intended it to be. God threatens judgment on those who would pervert the display of His image in this divinely designed expression of love: *fornicators and adulterers God will judge*. Of course the implication is that He approves and honors those who are sexually pure, who honor marriage and keep sexual intercourse undefiled.

We not only have God's perspective on marriage, but in 1 Corinthians 7.2-5, we also learn that marriage is God's provision:

> *But because of immoralities, let each man have his own wife, and let each woman have her own husband. Let the husband fulfill his duty to his wife, and likewise the wife to her husband. The wife does not have authority over her own body, but the husband does; and likewise also, the husband does not have authority over his own body, but the wife does. Stop depriving one another, except by agreement for a time that you may devote yourselves to prayer, and come together again lest Satan tempt you because of your lack of self-control.*

God has given provision. In verse 2, marital sexual intimacy is the divine provision in view of the prevalence of immoralities and illicit sexual activity. Paul says, *Let each have their own – have* is a term implying sexual possession. The old marriage vows include the words, "to have and to hold." Those words express the privilege of sexual possession. 1 Corinthians 7.3 tells us that a husband and a wife are each reciprocally, mutually obligated to one another in matters of sexual intimacy. "Wait a minute," someone might say, "did you say 'mutual obligation'? This is a first century document. Isn't 'mutual obligation' a modern, post-women's lib view of sex? How could Paul have that perspective on sex? Wasn't Paul some rabbinic male chauvinist who just parroted the degrading views of women current in his day?" Apparently not. Paul was obviously not parroting his culture. He was penning the words of God. Mutual obligation: what a liberating idea for first century women! Women had no rights in Paul's culture. In the Greco-Roman culture of Paul's day, to come to a married couple and address the wife and say, "Dear lady, his body is yours. You have rights over him. He has a dutiful obligation to you," would be radical. But gospel love is radical, and biblical. In Deuteronomy 24.5, a young newly-wed man whom the military had conscripted would not go off to war for a year. Instead, he would stay at home and learn *how to please his wife* - a radical, but biblical concept.

Normally, a spouse is not to deprive the other of sexual satisfaction (verse 5), but the couple can agree to relinquish that delightful privilege as a form of religious fasting. Yet Paul warns against the dangers of asceticism and does not want couples to tolerate a sexual distance in marriage. They might not be able to achieve the pious purposes of a sexual fast amid the rising pressure of sexual desire. The couple's *lack of self-control* could make them vulnerable to satanic temptation despite their noble intent for the fast. If a couple is not being sexually intimate in a mutually acceptable and regular cadence, they make themselves vulnerable to an assault from Satan. In this day of heightened sexual stimuli and disintegrating sexual restraint, we need to honor the marriage bed and frequent it according to the mutual needs, rights and desires of both spouses.

Discussion Questions for Chapter Eleven:
The Challenge of Unbiblical Communication Patterns

1. Why are words so important in light of Creation, the Fall, and Redemption?

2. Why is the man especially accountable for words? What are the three kinds of words that Adam was responsible for before Eve was fashioned and what did those words define

3. Adam is “the Definer.” How did Adam exercise this stewardship and what are some implications for us today?

4. According to Ephesians 5.6, how is a husband to sanctify his wife?

5. How should a Christian husband exercise his stewardship of words?

6. What, according to Willard Harley, is a woman’s greatest need and how do a husband’s words meet that need?

7. How does the woman’s need for affection interplay with the man’s need for sexual intimacy?

8. How do the “four guiding stars” factor into our understanding of sexual intimacy?

9. According to Hebrews 13.4, what is God’s attitude toward sexual intimacy?

10. What are some implications of Paul’s words in 1 Corinthians 7.2-5?

12

The Challenge of Unavoidable Death

Married to my wife

We desire to develop deeper marital intimacy over the course of a lifetime of gospel love with our spouse. Yet, as we age, we experience the accelerating decay of the outer man (2 Corinthians 4.16), and we experience the creeping advance of death. Death, by definition, effects separation. Death severs the unions of life. We face the challenge of striving for deeper unity and intimacy while death is simultaneously working to pull us apart and eventually separate us. How can we develop deeper intimacy over the course of a lifetime while we continually experience the decay of the outer man? What will motivate us to engage in the work of communicating gospel love while experiencing that unavoidable pull that dust has on these bodies of dust?

Peter answers that question by directing the husband to love his wife as she is defined by creation and redemption (1 Peter 3.7). In the first part of the verse, the husband is to love his wife under the direction of the guiding star of creation. *You husbands, likewise, live with your wives in an understanding way, as with the weaker vessel, since she is a woman*. Peter tells us that *she is a woman*. That is what Adam called his wife in Genesis 2.23. God's creation purposes still determine our understanding of the genders and the original created order still regulates our marriages.

Peter commands the husband to *live with her*. The word he uses means "cohabit." In other words, spend time with her. It is not good for the man to be alone (Genesis 2.18). We need companionship. Socialize together. Be together. I know we are all busy. We live here, we take the kids to school over there, we worship back over there, and we work way over there and take business trips all over the place! Modern living can impose geographical separation on us. Beware: we must not allow a busy lifestyle to force us to go separate ways and live separate lives. Peter says *live with her*. Be in the same location with her. Spend time with her.

Time? Spend time with her? Where can we grab time in our hectic, busy, modern lifestyles? Is Peter's command practical for the frenzied, frantic pace of modern life? We might be tempted to think that this voice from the first century is irrelevant to the realities of the twenty-first century. "Spend time with her"? How? I am not unfamiliar with the demands of twenty-first century American busyness. We live a half hour to an hour's drive from anything we do and have to coordinate the schedules of a family of six. I live in my daily calendar almost as much as in my Bible! Peter wants me to enjoy a healthy, Christ-honoring marriage and he says, "Spend time with her." I look at my date book and wonder: "When?"

If the command to spend time with your wife challenges you, let me recommend that you consider the first principle of biblical time-management: the Lord's Day. The blessing of the Lord's Day can compensate for the time depletions of busy lifestyles. The Sabbath has been made for man (Mark 2.27). God has given you a regular time for refreshment in His presence and commanded you to order your schedule to receive the blessing of God's rejuvenating presence. A judicious use of the Lord's Day will go a long way to insuring that you spend time with her as you order your schedules to spend time with the Lord on His day.

Peter elaborates further, *live with her in an understanding way*. We get the word "science" from the Greek word translated *understanding*. In other words, Peter is telling men to observe their wives and employ the scientific method! Study her. Get the correct data and discover just who it is that you have married. I have not married an institution. I am not married to "marriage." I have married a woman. And I have not married just any woman: I have married this particular woman. So I must study her. I must weigh and measure and understand her if I would know how to cherish and nurture her as *a weaker vessel*. The concern here is for her physical well-being. The word *vessel* refers to her bodily needs which make her *weaker*, or more delicate as *a woman*. She is a fragile porcelain vase, whereas I am more like a metal bucket. She is *a woman* and I must understand who and what she is as God created her. The guiding star of creation directs my responsibilities as a Christian husband.

Married to my sister

Peter, having urged us to love our wives to fulfill God's creation purposes, then commands us to love with redemptive purpose. We are to *grant her honor as a fellow heir of the grace of life so that your prayers may not be hindered*. Peter tells us to *grant her honor*. This was a Greek idiom, a common way of speaking that meant to give value and worth to something. What value and worth are we to give our Christian wives? *Grant her honor as a fellow heir of the grace of life*. She is your wife in this age and she is your sister in the age to come. As your sister in Christ, she is just as saved as you are. She is just as blessed as you are. In Christ *there is neither male nor female* (Galatians 3.28). In Christ, she is your spiritual equal, your sister in the Lord.

Grant her honor. Respect her for the exercise of her spiritual gifts. She has received endowments of the Spirit, gifts and graces which God designed to work to edify her brethren, in this verse, her husband. Give place to her insight and counsel. Build a pulpit in your marriage that is equally accessible to either one of you, from which both of you can address each other's conscience with an open Bible. You will not find my wife preaching from the pulpit in the church of which we are members. But as my spiritual sister, she has every right to open the Scripture and address me from the pulpit that we have built in our marriage. I am not saying that as my spiritual sister, she is warranted to ignore the principles of headship, but rather that she, as my helper and my sister, shares in the stewardship of our love. When she brings the Word to bear on an issue, I am to honor her as one who is my spiritual equal. She speaks to me as her brother in Christ, who is yet her husband in this creation. She is of the same body of Christ with me, and the responsibilities that we have as members of the same church are heightened within the bounds of our marriage. She is a member of Christ and Christ has given her to me to minister His love to me. Here the guiding star of redemption directs us.

Why are we, as Christian husbands, to understand and to

love our wives according to creation and redemption? Because our intimacy with our wives conditions our intimacy with Christ: s*o that your prayers may not be hindered*. Gentlemen, you cannot cultivate communion with Christ unless you are fostering intimacy with your wife. It is impossible to commune with Christ if you are not communicating with your wife. He has made you to be one flesh with her, and when you pray, He knows you in your union with your wife. It is as though when we approach Christ in prayer, He asks, "So, how are things with the missus?" If things are not well, those things will cause spiritual static in our prayers and hinder our fellowship with Christ Himself. *If therefore you are presenting your offering at the altar, and there remember that your brother has something against you, leave your offering there before the altar, and go your way; first be reconciled to your brother, and the come and present your offering* (Matthew 5.23-24). As Christian husbands, we arc not going to grow in Christ without cultivating intimacy with our wives.

Discipleship - "Until death do us part"

Peter's words encompass time and eternity. A husband is to know and love his wife as she is in her womanhood, defined by this present created order. We are also to know and love our wives as she is *a fellow-heir of the grace of life* and a fellow citizen with us in the eternal Kingdom of God. Peter wants us to love our wives with a love that spans creation and eternity, past and future. But there is something that occurs between our experiences of these two parts of the verse. There is an event that transpires between my experiences of being married to this woman in this present age and knowing her as my eternal sibling in the age to come. There is something that happens between my life in this creation and in the eternal Kingdom. What separates the two? The great separator: death.

Many of us have included those familiar words "until death do us part" in our wedding vows. Death will indeed part us, for *when they rise from the dead, they neither marry nor are given in marriage but are like angels in heaven* (Mark 12.25). Marriage is not an eternal institution. Marriage is an arrangement designed for this present world order and it ends with our death. It is part of this passing age and this age is already passing away (1 John 2.17). Death is already nipping at our heels and the time for marital intimacy is fleeting away. If we are going to be intimate and know each other in a celebration of gospel love we have to do it now, we have to do it urgently, we have to do it passionately.

Encroaching death advances. Whatever my wife and I can be in the intimacy of our one flesh, we must be that – now. Inevitable death approaches with an ever-quickening cadence. As death comes nearer, I get more frantic. I want to know my wife and to be known by her immediately. I cannot postpone the summons of love. I cannot allow unresolved tensions to fester and corrode our intimacy. The time I have spent procrastinating when I should have been confessing and forgiving is wasted, irretrievable time. Let not sin deplete the already far too little time we have. The nearer death comes, the more it pushes me to get even closer, even more intimately connected to my dearest earthly companion to whom I will be married for far too brief a time.

We take out pictures and look at ourselves as we were thirty years ago. We look at ourselves now. We can see death approaching. The bodies with which we are one flesh are decaying: the loss of hearing, the loss of teeth, the loss of endurance, the loss of youthful muscle tone and skin tone, the loss of vitality.

I sometimes look at my hands and have this disconnect experience. That is my grandfather's hand! Why is that hand sticking out of the end of my sleeve? What is that tissue paper wrinkly stuff on the back of my hand? It is death. It is nipping and chewing. It is already having an effect on us. It is sending shots over the bow. It is announcing its impending arrival.

In spite of this intimacy that we are so frantically trying to knit together in these fleeting days, death is coming, death is near, death has arrived and it intends is to separate us. That is what death does: it separates. But we are in Christ. *Death is swallowed up in victory. O death, where is your victory? O death, where is your sting?* (1 Corinthians 15.54-55). We love each other with gospel love. We paradoxically pursue life and intimacy amid and through the suffocating presence of death. We find self-fulfillment through self-sacrifice and service directed towards one another. We live out our discipleship in our marriage, taking up our cross daily, denying self, dying to sin, that we might live to God as those alive from the dead (Romans 6.13). We triumph over death in Christ. As husband and wife we are fellow heirs of grace, eternal brothers and sisters in Christ. But because we are in Christ, though we die, yet shall we live (John 11.25-26).

In ways that I cannot understand, my wife is my flesh, and we are one. My discipleship, my pursuit of Christ, now lies buried inside her. As I respond to Christ's call to die to self, I learn to bury myself into her, and there, in intimacy with my wife, I find expanding communion with Christ. In union with her, I experience unhindered prayer. She conditions my "narrow way," my path of obedience to Christ. In her lies the path of my discipleship. I follow Christ as I learn to love her. She, by her love, gives me reason to hope that redeemed sinners *can* love each other! I already begin to experience something of that love that will permeate the community of the redeemed in the age to come. As we love each other with gospel love, as we experience the one flesh intimacy of symphonic souls, we have a foretaste of what human relationships will be like in the consummated Kingdom. Already, by the power of the Spirit, my *fellow heir of the grace of life* and I have begun to know each other in the way that we will know each other for all eternity. Already, by the down payment of the Spirit, we have begun to experience something of life after death, of that life that conquers death. *O death, where is your victory* (1 Corinthians 15.55)?

Death will not be victorious. *He who believes in Me shall live even if he dies* (John 11.25). And we will die, should the Lord tarry. And when we die, our marriage will end. Encroaching death looms before us and we know that one day death will separate us. But how can we be separated when the nature of our union is so embedded in Christ? How can we be separated when the path of our discipleship to Christ is found in our marital intimacy?

We are dying and death will one day come and separate us. *He who believes in Me shall live even if he dies, and everyone who lives and believes in Me shall never die* (John 11.25-26). Can I apply these words to my marriage? Can I be bold to think that Tricia and I will be united even if we are separated? Are we not united in Jesus in an eternal union which can never be fully and finally severed? Yes. In Christ, we are eternally united. Marriage as an institution is bound to this created order and it is completed in death and will end with the passing of this age, but Christ has infused our marriage with gospel love and with the life of the age to come. We will not be married in the new heavens and the new earth, but we are already experiencing a "new creation" kind of love in our marriage and that love will continue, even though our marriage will end. Although Tricia and I will not be married in eternity, we are nevertheless joint heirs of the grace of life, eternally joined together as members of Christ. Indeed, we will be joined with the entire community of the redeemed as members of Christ.

A SOCIETY OF LOVE

In this age, marriage is an institution within which we experience intimacy as we learn to love each other with gospel love. In this little society of two, we experience that love which triumphs over sin and the threat of death. As we practice this love in our marriage, we learn how to train our children in this same gospel love. We then strive to transfer the attitudes and skills we cultivate in our home to the society of the church where gospel love must also characterize our ecclesiastical relationships. In the age to come, the society of love will expand to its God-intended perfection. In the age to come gospel love, new creation love, will characterize, not a society of two, or a society of six, or one hundred. Sinless, triumphant, resurrection love will be known throughout that perfected society which no man will be able to number. The glorified society of the redeemed from every tribe, tongue, people, and nation will live in eternal love. There the Spirit will intimately unite us with all the perfected people of God from all the ages. All in that saved society will enjoy an intimate love which the most mature Christian marriage can barely taste on this side of the resurrection. There we will know the full meaning of what it means to be the bride of Christ and to have Jesus Himself as our eternal husband. In the conquest of the final resurrection, love will conquer all sin and banish death. Tricia and I, by the grace of God, will be among that perfected society of love. Scripture gives us every reason to believe that we will know each other in heaven and we will discover that our Lord used our marital intimacy to sanctify us and to prepare us for eternity. We will learn that our marriage was God's training ground to prepare us to live in a glorified society in which gospel love has triumphed.

I sometimes think of that perfected society of intimacy when I visit big cities. Cities are so impersonal. You move along the current in a crowd of people, flowing across sidewalks, through turnstiles, up escalators, like nameless cells in huge veins, coursing through a body made of cement. Cities are so oppressively overwhelming, so impersonal, and so mechanical, as people press against each other with no real living connection. Think of what it will be like in that *city which has foundations, whose architect and builder is God* (Hebrews 11.10). Think of life in *the holy city, new Jerusalem made ready as a bride adorned for her husband* (Revelation 21.2). Think of seeing people milling about on the heavenly streets and knowing them, each one of them, knowing all of them intimately with an intimate love far greater than that to which the best of marriages could ever attain! No, Tricia and I will not need to be married then. Yet, I imagine being with her in heaven. I think of knowing her then, not as my wife, but as my sister, my fellow-heir of grace. I hope to hear her tell me of how my love for her, my headship in our marriage, was used by our Lord to bring her to her eternal home. What love will we then know when we will finally perceive how the Lord knit the thread of our marriage into the tapestry of His perfect plan? How will we then rejoice to see the drops of our marital intimacy blend into the eternal ocean of His love? Our marriage will have accomplished God's purpose as a harbinger of heaven. Our marriage, a loving society of two, points to that perfected society, the society of the bride of the Lamb.

Even so, come Lord Jesus

But more than preparing me to live in eternal loving union with you, my redeemed brethren, my marriage is instructing me to live in union with Jesus. We are to love Jesus more than we love our wife or husband, and our love for our spouse is one way in which we can express our love for Jesus. It is only Jesus who gives me the love with which I love my wife, enabling me to love her in a way that shows my love for my Lord. As I embrace her, I turn from her, to Him. *If anyone comes to Me, and does not hate his own father and mother and wife and children and brothers and sisters, yes, and even his own life, he cannot be My disciple* (Luke 14.26). By loving my wife, I seek to follow my Lord. In His eternal embrace, I triumph over death. In union with Him, I cannot ultimately be separated from anything or any one who is likewise united to my conquering King.

Even as I strain to see these glories *in a mirror dimly* (1 Corinthians 13.12), my heart aches because I know that between now and then, death will overwhelm us. Unless Jesus returns first, one of us will stand at the grave of the other and death will part us. Yet, such is the context in which we live out our discipleship to Christ. We take up our cross daily (Luke 9.23). We die daily (1 Corinthians 15.31). Discipleship is following Christ into death. Faith is grasping onto promises that our Lord will fulfill only on the other side of death. Faith lays hold of resurrection realities. My marriage will not endure beyond this present age, but our love will. Not only will it endure, it will explode in its immensity as Christ joins us to Him and to all His people in eternal intimacy and joy.

So as death approaches, as we experience the decaying demise of the outer man, we follow Christ into death. We will not give up. We will not yield to mere fleshly weakness. We will yet strive to demonstrate our discipleship to Christ in our marriage, until death do us part. We know that death's parting is but a passage into a more glorious intimacy of eternal love, perfected and enjoyed by all the saints in union with our Head, Christ Jesus our Lord. O how I earnestly desire to love my wife with more intimacy! Indeed, I long to love the brethren and to be loved with the love of Christ. It is with that yearning that I embrace my wife and pray, *Even so, come, Lord Jesus!* (Revelation 22.20)

Discussion Questions for Chapter Twelve:
The Challenge of Unavoidable Death

1. What is the challenge posed by "unavoidable death"?

2. How does 1 Peter 3.7a reinforce the original creation duties given to us as husbands?

3. What the duty of the husband in 1 Peter 3.7a and how can we fulfill that duty in our hectic busy lifestyles?

4. What other creation duty does Peter enforce in 1 Peter 3.7a and why?
5. What redemption duty does Peter enforce in 1 Peter 3.7b?
6. What is involved in granting our believing wives honor?
7. Why are we as Christian husbands to love our wives according to creation and redemption?
8. Is it possible for a Christian husband to enjoy fellowship with Christ when he is not cultivating intimacy with his wife?
9. What event occurs between the first and second halves of 1 Peter 3.7?
10. Why is the development of intimacy an urgent need?
11. What does gospel love allow us as married Christians to experience
12. Marriage will end in death but death will not be the end of what?
13. From what does "the society of love" emerge and grow?
14. God uses marriage as a training ground to prepare us for what?
15. How do you envision meeting your spouse in the age to come?
16. Who is ultimately loved when we love our spouse intimately with gospel love?

Notes

[1] I do not intend to imply that a single, unmarried person is not “the image of God.” We image God as individual humans. The unmarried Jesus is “image of God” (compare Colossians 1.15) and He validates the legitimacy of celibate singleness for His people (Matthew 19.12). The phrase “image of God” is also used in Scripture to speak of a filial relationship, a relationship of sonship. Certainly single Christians are “sons of God” as are their married brethren.

[2] This is the answer to the first question of the Westminster Shorter Catechism: “What is the chief end of man?”

[3] Here we see how a single man (or woman) is the true image of God. A study of Adam in Genesis 2 yields much insight for the single Christian. As Adam matures, he is given responsibilities for creation, for words, for worship and for others.

[4]Although the Hebrew word *adam* has been used throughout Genesis 1 and 2 to identify ‘the man,’ the KJV transliterates that word into the man’s proper name ‘Adam’ in Genesis 2.19 and the NIV and NASB in Genesis 2.20. Interestingly, the translators give the man his name in conjunction with the naming of the animals and the woman. ‘Adam’ is a more generic term similar to ‘human.’ ‘Man’ (Hebrew *ish*) in verse 23 is used more of a particular individual man and is used later in Scripture as ‘husband.’

[5] Mike Mason, *The Mystery of Marriage* (Sisters, Oregon: Multnomah Books, 1985), 100. Mason offers insightful, and often poetically profound, observations.

[6] Cf. Job 15.31; Jeremiah 37.9; 1 Corinthians 3.18, 6.9; 15.33; Galatians 6.3, 7; James 1.16, 26; 1 John 1.8

[7] The definition of the term *propitiation* is debated among theologians. The classic traditional definition means "the turning away of wrath by an offering." Some modern (read "liberal"?) theologians prefer to speak only of "expiation" (the removal of sin) and deny that this term refers to the wrath of God. But Scripture is clear that sin incurs divine wrath and that God's wrath is propitiated, appeased, satisfied, by the atoning death of Jesus Christ, the sacrifice graciously given and made by God Himself.

[8] *You are the salt of the earth; but if the salt has become tasteless, how will it be made salty again? It is good for nothing any more, except to be thrown out and trampled under foot by men* (Matthew 5.13).

[9] "Common grace" is that benevolent goodness which God bestows on all creation which yet falls short of "saving grace" by which sinners are brought into union with Christ. God exercises His common grace as He patiently postpones deserved punishment and restrains sin through the institutions of the family, the state, and the influence of the church upon the collective conscience of a culture. God exercises common grace by sustaining all creaturely life and by enabling men, even though they are not savingly joined to Christ, to yet do much that is morally good in itself. The ultimate expression of God's common grace is demonstrated as the church proclaims the gospel to all men everywhere, calling all to repentance and faith in Jesus Christ.

[10] This interpretation of Feminism is also the thesis of Mary Kassian, *The Feminist Gospel:The Movement to Unite Feminism with the Church*, (Wheaton, Illinois, Crossway Books. 1992).

[11] Greek dictionaries of Greek words

[12] For an extensive study of this assertion, see Wayne Grudem's research in Appendix #1, in George W. Knight, *Role Relationship of Men and Women*, (Moody Press, Chicago, 1985)

[13] If you have your Bible handy, you would do well to open it to

Ephesians 5.21 and follow along as I attempt to exegete (interpret accurately) this passage.

[14] To read 'into the text' is call eisegesis ("eis" in Greek means "into"). Exegesis ("ex" in Greek means "out of") is the endeavor to derive the meaning of the text out of the text. See footnote 13.

[15] Gilbert Bilezikian, *Beyond Sex Roles: What the Bible Says About a Woman's Place in Church and Family* (Grand Rapids, Baker, 1985), 153 ff. Cited in Peter T. O'Brien, *The Letter to the Ephesians* (Pillar Commentary, Grand Rapids, Eerdmans, 1999), 401

[16] Mike Mason, *The Mystery of Marriage* (Sisters, Oregon: Multnomah, 1985), 183-184.

[17] Peter O'Brien, *The Letter to the Ephesians* (Grand Rapids, Michigan: Eerdmanns), 411-412.

[18] See 1 Timothy 5.21; Hebrews 1.6;12.22,23

[19] See Galatians 2.15 where *nature* is used to speak of Jewish culture.

[20] See Romans 1.25; 2.14 where *nature* refers to creation morality.

[21] Although see Proverbs 17.6.

[22] Fritz Rienecker and Cleon Rogers, *A Linguistic Key to the Greek New Testament,* (Grand Rapids, MI. Zondervan, 1976), 549.

[23] Ibid, 549.

[24] Willard F. Harley, Jr., *His Needs Her Needs: Building An Affair-proof Marriage* (Grand Rapids, Michigan: Fleming H. Revell, 1986), 32.

[25] Ibid, 34

[26] Ibid, 39

[27] Ibid, 40

[28] Ibid, 38

[29] Ibid, 38